JACK'S WAR

JACK'S WAR

The diary and drawings of
JACK HALSTEAD
- a Great War survivor

STREETS PUBLISHERS
Baldock, England.

First published in 2005 by
Streets Publishers, Royston Road, Baldock, Herts SG7 6NW

Copyright © Streets Publishers and Royston & District Museum

ISBN: 0 9546698 5 1

Designed and Printed in England by
Streets Printers, Royston Road, Baldock, Herts SG7 6NW

ACKNOWLEDGEMENT

The publishers would like to acknowledge the immense help and
co-operation they have received from the many people who have
been involved in the production of this book.

They would especially like to extend their thanks to the staff,
members and friends of Royston & District Museum and
Royston Town Council.

Contents

Introduction

Christopher John Edward Halstead, known as Jack, joined the Army in November 1915 at the age of 18 years and became a gunner.

He was posted to France in March 1917 and for the next two–and–a–half years fought from the Somme to Ypres, Lens and back to the Somme. During this time he was wounded and gassed several times and on his 21st birthday he was fighting for his life in Noreuil.

He entered Germany with the Army of Occupation, where he remained until he was demobbed in 1919 after which he returned to Royston where he worked until the day of his death in 1963.

A quiet man, he chose not to take part in the everyday activities of the town. His hobbies were sketching, photography, gardening and bee-keeping; and he was an enthusiastic supporter of promoting Esperanto as he believed it would improve international understanding and thus reduce the likelihood of another world war.

History proved otherwise and in the Second World War, Jack served as a volunteer fire–fighter while his wife Josie worked as a controller for the fire service.

Jack retired in 1960 from the hardware business his father and a partner had established in 1903 in Market Hill, Royston.

He returned to help in the shop on Monday, December 16, 1963 and was found in the yard at the back of the shop, having suffered a fatal heart attack.

A gifted amateur artist, Jack had been encouraged by Royston artist EH Whydale to continue sketching, but Jack's father disapproved and insisted upon him working in the family business. If Jack resented this, it did not deter him from sketching: the youth of his generation had been lost in fighting the war and his self–imposed isolation was possibly the result of his experiences, but somehow he found the strength to illustrate his diary.

The diary is a testament to his immense skill at depicting the grim reality and the humourous tales of life in the trenches during the war to end all wars.

Transcription

Transcribing this diary has been a great privilege. One of the most striking things is Jack Halstead's complete lack of self pity and his ability to make the best of the situation in which he found himself. He is one of the many genuine heroes of war, most of whom are forgotten. He suffered from vermin and being both gassed and wounded. He worked in conditions of discomfort and horror that nobody would ever want to experience. Many of his friends were cut down beside him. He did not glorify his situation in any way, and he did not hate the opposing forces. He got on well with his former enemies when he was with the occupying forces in Germany. These experiences affected not only him, but also his whole generation.

This diary was transcribed as it was written. Jack Halstead intended his diary to be read and lent it to any person who expressed an interest in reading it. For this reason he copied his entire war diary from the many small notebooks and bits of paper on which he had written the original. Many of them were crumpled, bloodstained and muddy and partially legible or perhaps legible only to him. Some of the original illustrations were cut from the original and stuck on the page. He copied the others when he wrote his "good" copy. He also added some corrections, which may not be visible in the facsimile, as they were written very lightly in pencil.

I would like to thank F. John Smith and Carole Kaszak for proof reading this diary. If there are mistakes, they are all mine. We are indebted to the Halstead family for permitting this poignant diary to be published.

Jane Vincent
Curator, Royston and District Museum 1991-2003

Jack Halstead was an ordinary young man in the Royston of the early 1900s whose life was changed beyond belief with the outbreak of war in 1914. He joined the Royal Field Artillery on the 1 November 1915 and served in France and Germany until 1919.

There are many books about the Great War written by senior officers and politicians but very few written by ordinary soldiers. This is a remarkable, contemporaneous record of what life was like at the "sharp end" of the war.

I expect that he knew most of those whose names fill the panels of the War Memorial in Royston.

A. R. Smith
Lieutenant Colonel (Rtd).

Glossary

I have changed abbreviations into their full names to prevent the necessity of having numerous footnotes. I am grateful to Colonel Ray Smith, and the library staff of the Imperial War Museum and "Firepower" for help in deciphering or confirming them.

The most frequently used abbreviation is S.O.S

In this context it means that when not firing, the guns were laid or pointed to a specific area which was regarded as dangerous and therefore a target. In the event of an attack or other order to start firing, the guns would be ready. The infantry would signal S.O.S by flares, telephone or wireless, and the guns would then respond immediately.

Gun crews had to be ready at all times to respond to signals, so there was always someone on S.O.S duty. However, on 21st March 1918, The observation posts had been overrun and the signallers at Jack's position and the forward positions were dead, wounded or captured. The gun crew therefore, were firing at a point given to them earlier which was no longer a danger. At this stage of the battle, the whole of that sector was drenched with gas, and pulverised by artillery and liquid fire. All the crew could do was keep firing, and hope they were doing the right thing.

A gun team *consisted of six horses,* **the Limber** *(cart carrying shells, tools, feed for the horses etc,) and the gun. Jack Halstead as Limber gunner looked after the horses and the Limber. However during the battles, he did all the work of a gunner.*

Drivers. *In the context of the artillery of the period, a driver rode one of the lead horses.*

Other frequently mentioned items are **"Gothas"** *(German Bombers) and* **"captive balloons"**. *On the Western Front, they were used for observation. The balloon would rise, but remain anchored to the ground by cables. Observers would then be able to see enemy troop movements and direct the gunners. Curiously enough, the first parachutes were issued to the observers in the balloons and it was a while before they were issued to pilots of aeroplanes.*

"Bivi" is an abbreviation of "bivouac" and it is a sort of tent or shelter made from whatever materials the soldiers found at hand.

Elephant Iron is heavy galvanised corrugated iron. It was much in demand for making shelters and lining dugouts.

B.E.F. is another frequently used abbreviation. It means "British Expeditionary Force".

Jack Halstead describes the terrible noise of **a barrage**, which meant that all the enemy artillery was directed to a specific part of the front. In addition there would also be a hail of machine gun bullets, "liquid fire" and usually gas as well.

"Shell Shock". This was the psychological result of the continuous gunfire and the conditions in the trenches. On September 23-4th 1917, Jack describes how one of the gunners reacted to shell shock.

The wounded too in the primitive conditions suffered gas gangrene, rabies and other appalling complaints from the contaminated mud. Even to this day the ground around Ypres and other major battlefields still carries dangerous bacteria, and the now wooded areas of the conflict in Flanders have the highest incidence of rabies in foxes.

JV

MY EXPERIENCES IN FRANCE, FLANDERS AND GERMANY 1917-1919

Under the above heading I reproduce the diary which I wrote when on active service. A few more details than in the original. The maps too are copied from the original. Not copied from genuine maps, but as I saw the surroundings when at the various positions.

Keeping such a diary as this, I guess was against all the rules and regulations. If I had been captured no doubt it would have interested the enemy.

This copy will give the reader a slight idea as to what modern war is like - just a slight idea. Some of the experiences it is quite impossible to portray in their full colours. For example who can on paper or any other way give the realistic touch to the average night in Pilken Ridge (in the Ypres salient) a night as long as any week with its death-trap roads, gas, mud, shrieking shells. How can one describe them.

Still there were good times and really by taking the rough times with the smooth, we didn't fare badly. Whichever it was, one always found us in the same mood making the best of it. Always a smile in the tightest corner and I may say that E. sub of the 295 Brigade were

Timeline: 1917

The First World War spanned four years and involved many nation states.

This section lists the events of the year 1917, the fourth year of the war. This year saw the adoption by the German high command of the disastrous policy of unrestricted submarine warfare - disastrous in that it brought about America's entry into the war within the space of a couple of months, and ultimately led to her downfall the following year.

Meanwhile the British launched a major offensive at Passchendaele in autumn 1917: as at the Somme the previous year it proved a highly costly failure. 1917 also saw Russia's exit from the war amid two revolutions, the first in February and a second in October.

renowned for their "making the best of it" mood — thanks perhaps to those in charge.

Now for a few items that might be of interest:

One reads tales of men living for months on a desert island — of men sent into exile — One might imagine that the life for them was dull. One can compare such cases with life in "the line". (Line was the term used by artillerymen for the gun line, or where the guns were in action). I can assure you that such a life was far from dull. To begin with, there was plenty of work. The firing, the unloading of ammunition, carrying it to the gun pits, making "dumps" for the shells, digging trenches, gunpit digging, digging "saps" (or tunnels), dugouts, general cleaning up and we were always improving our positions both for safety and comfort. And we also had our recreation. It's true there was not much to do, but time never hung. Card playing, telling yarns, arguments, letter writing, singing, and reading. Books were scarce — a book generally did the round of the battery. Newspapers were always thoroughly read. In the summer we made good use of a ball. A walk to a neighbouring battery made a change. These walks were often disturbed

by enemy shelling – sometimes the walks were
compulsory. Water both for washing and drinking
had to be carried as far as two miles – perhaps a
walk to get supplies at a canteen. Clothes we had
to wash. Not an interesting occupation as we
couldn't hang the clothes out to dry, as we should
have wished. We were always under German
observation. To hang clothes out would be
dangerous. Then was the daily task of decreasing
the army of insects (known as Chats or lice) that
infested our clothes. These small-game hunts just
had to be. This too was far from a pleasant
occupation especially in cold weather. Plenty of
sport – without exception one can say that every
soldier in France slaughtered at least 500 of
these pests. When we were fed up with the
slaughter, we would go the shirts again. You may
laugh, but it was far from a laughing matter.
Without these daily hunts, sleep would be
impossible. The garment would be boiled, soaked
in petrol, soaked in disinfectant, but next day
they were as thick as ever.

As to food:

At some places we fared badly but not often.
Meals were regular and plain. Plenty of stew and
biscuits. No one ever looked bad on these rations.

These are the rations of the average day:

8.30 a.m.

Porridge or "Bengoo"

1 pint of tea

1/4 loaf of bread or ten biscuits.
   (More often the latter)

Dinner 1 p.m

Stew or boiled mutton and potatoes.

Tea 5 p.m

1 pint of tea.

1/4 lb. bread or two biscuits.

Jam (1lb for 4 or 5)

Or cheese

Supper we had to provide. We always managed to find something. And we always managed to scrounge some tea or cocoa for a drink when on night firing.

Cigarettes

We had a weekly ration of 20 cigarettes and a box of matches. Many a time we were without either.

Rum

During the winter, we had a daily ration and often it was a liberal ration. On rough fronts, we had two or three rations. We always had a reserve supply. Water bottles full and in one place a petrol can full.

In the summer we had lime juice in place of rum. It was then that our own reserves came in handy. Without this rum, many would have gone under. Although we were often soaked through with rain - wading through seas of mud, colds were practically unknown.

And when out at rest. How nice it was to get back to a civilised village once again; and we made the best of our rests. What lively nights we spent at these little estaminets. Music - beer – one could drink gallons of French beer. One would term it "spoilt water" If a man went out with the intention of drowning himself and then happened to be handy to a vat of French beer he would think twice before jumping in. Vin rouge and vin blanc was plentiful, and champagne too could be bought for 5 francs. Coffee we had in plenty. Egg and chips was our favourite dish for supper. What times we had. Something to look forward to when in the line.

These were the wishes of a soldier in France.

1. A comfortable place to sleep in
2. A smoke
3. Food.

That was the order of the day.

A comfortable resting-place always topped the list. Many a time we were in bed by 7 p.m and no matter how rough the bed was, it was always hard to roll out in the mornings.

Pay

When in action, paydays were few, but we made up for it when again in civilisation. To use the old army phrase: "We don't get much money, but we do see life". Yes, a shilling (5 pence) a day was the pay. Still one in France could live cheaply. Cigarettes were about ten pence for 50(about .04p) and one litre of beer was 2 pence. (About one penny in to-days currency)

As to lights:

When in action it was a daily ration of one candle for each dugout, but believe me we always looked after ourselves and always had a good supply by us.

WITH B BATTERY
295 BRIGADE 59TH DIVISION

13th March 1917

A cold frosty morning. At an early hour we left our headquarters at <u>Lark Hill</u>. With full kit, marched to <u>Adesbury</u> (a small village on the edge of the Plain). At 9 a.m all guns, horses and kit were loaded on the troop train. We arrived at <u>Southampton</u> at 11 a.m. Then came the busy time of loading all our belongings on to the boat. The guns were hauled on board with little cranes and the horses and mules were either pulled or pushed up the narrow gangway. These animals were as awkward as ever they could be. The first boat left at 5 p.m and we followed by a light passenger boat. Passed the Isle of Wight and seaplane base. The M(a)uritania just coming in. Not a very joyful crowd. There was not much rejoicing on such occasions. Some started singing some rather appropriate songs some containing these words" It may be for years and it may be forever". Well the songsters soon quietened down. We stood on deck until dark and then retired below deck and were soon asleep.

March 1

Zimmermann Telegram published in US press, which detailed the alledged German Proposal of Alliance with Mexico

March 11

British capture Baghdad

March 12

US President Woodrow Wilson announces arming of US merchantmen by executive order after failing to win approval from Congress

14th March

I should like to think that we arrived at Le Havre just after midnight but we slept on until 6 a.m. Awakened rather roughly by a crowd of Frenchmen selling postcards and French boys begging biscuits. A noisy crowd but I remember that we were very much interested and amused. We managed to get a wash on a destroyer that drew up at the side of our boat and I guess that we needed it. We then had a walk round the docks and later unloaded our cargo from the other boat. Rain. The drivers took charge of the horses. Guns were left at the docks. We marched up to number 2 camp Harfleur Put up horse lines. Our first experience of French mud. It was 10 p.m before we settled down. Rather rough sleeping twenty-three in a tent. Still it was cover, but although we were tired we did not get much sleep.

15th March

March 15

Tsar Nicholas II abdicates as a consequence of Russian Revolution

Packed up. I forget at what hour. Guess it was early. If we had to move off at 7 a.m we would be pulled out at 2 a.m. Why I don't know. Well on this occasion we moved off at 9 a.m. Collected the guns. Marched through streets to station. Everything was new and interesting to us.

Entrained. An awkward undertaking, on the
French Railways. Such awkward trucks. Many a
fall I have had when loading up. The men rode
thirty to a truck. And the horses, 8 in a truck,
four on each side facing the centre. A driver in
each truck to keep them quiet. Real lion tamers
they were!

Moved off at 12.30. What trains. Slow motion.
Very long and an engine at both ends. On every
four or five trucks rode a guard in a sort of
sentry box perched on the roof of a truck. This
guard at intervals when the train stopped would
run up and down blowing a sort of cow's horn.
Why he did so – well I don't know. Yes, very slow
these trains travelled. In fact when going up hills
we used to get out and walk and in that
manner we travelled, our legs hanging over the
side at the open door. Shouting perhaps some too
complimentary remarks to those that we saw
working in the fields and on the station
platforms. Whether they understood us, well lets
hope they didn't. Food during the journey
consisted of "Biscuits and Bully". On this
particular trip we halted at ----- (a wayside
station) for tea. Unusual. Perhaps they intended
to create a good impression. At dusk we settled
down to sleep.

16th March

Arrived at <u>Corbie</u> at 3 a.m and at once started unloading. No siding. Had to haul guns off with pulleys.

UNLOADING AT CORBIE.

Not a very pleasant game in the dark and a slow one. All manual work. Was 10 a.m before we moved off through <u>Corbie</u>. Quite a nice little town.

Arrived at <u>Hamelet</u>. Put up lines in orchard. Billet in barn. Then eight miles from Line. We were greatly interested in the gun flashes and the rumble like far off thunder of the guns. All spent the evening in little estaminet. sampled the beer and wine and exercising our knowledge of the French Language which I may say was small. Big Barrage on left front. Peronne fell that day.

17th March

Washed the guns down. River Somme was in flood at bottom of orchard. We had an argument as to

whether the water there had already passed
through the battlefield - the Somme area of
which we had heard so much. Whether it had we
never knew. Well it did not matter much. After
tea several of us walked into Corbie. Against all
the rules, still Corbie appeared rather attractive
so we risked it. We learned to risk a deal more
when more settled down to the life. An enjoyable
evening we had.

18th March

Right section moved off for action. They quite
believed that they were going into it. We were
then issued with box gas helmets. Our Major,
(Major O'Connell) said that they were our best
friends and they were too - At 11.30 a.m we
received orders to move up. Through Hamel and
then places that had once been villages to
Proyart. We were much interested in the
surroundings. Being new to us, it was sure to be
so. Trenches, dugouts, hundreds of graves just
marked with a bayonet, rifle or "tin hat".
(Mainly French graves) many with names
unknown. There were graves too of German
soldiers. It was about 4 p.m when we neared our
destination. We pulled into a field about 400
yards from the high road. Some road, nearly 3
feet of mud. Two general service wagons stuck. It
was then getting dark; we unhooked and left

them until the morning. We then walked over to our billets. These billets were in a wood. One could describe it as a huge rabbit warren. By the articles left, we learned that the previous occupants were Frenchmen. We scrounged round and found plenty of souvenirs. And some were useful. Trench boots etc., if we took everything that took our fancy well, we should have had some kit. The infantrymen always said that we had "ten men's kit". I confess that sometimes my kit was extra large. As limber gunner, I had opportunities of hiding surplus kit on the gun. Kits of the detachment too. Still my kit consisted of communal belongings such as cooking utensils etc. By the way, we were only supposed to have two blankets in winter and one in summer, but the gunners always had double the regulation issue. We slept well that night.

19th March

We made an inspection of dugouts. "Old Bill" said: " If you know a better 'ole, go to it" Well we did. A real "posh" place. Big stove and wire beds.

DUGOUT IN PROYART WOOD.

Just right for our detachment. We could have stuck it for the duration. Heard that the Germans had gone back.

20th March.

Snow. Awfully cold. Cleaned down the guns and they needed it after the muddy road.

Water had to be carried nearly half a mile. On guard at night. Snow was falling. Not an inviting night for a guard. A "bivi" we made with horse rugs. Made a good fire.

March 20

US President Woodrow Wilson's war cabinet votes unanimously in favour of declaring war on Germany

GUARD AT PROYART

In the distance we could hear the thunder of guns and flashes lit up the eastern sky. We talked and talked until daybreak. Too cold to sleep, we were wet with the falling snow, still this we did not notice when by the fire.

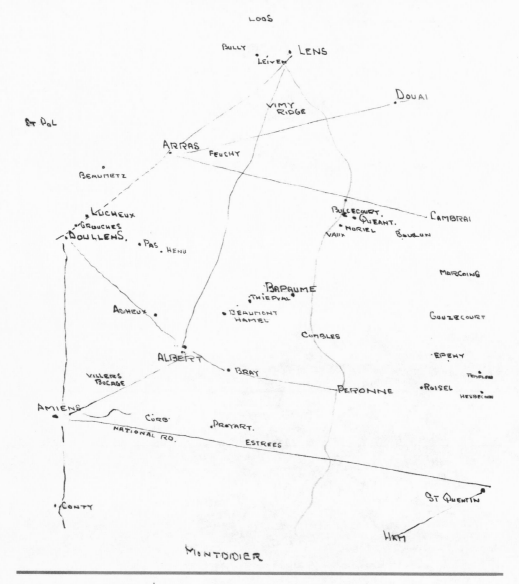

21st March

A quick move off. Supposed to relieve the 50th
Division (Northumbrian). Whether we did, I do
not know. Along the Great National Road
(Amiens to--?) we went, passing through
<u>Forocourt</u> and <u>Estrees</u>. What a wilderness it was.

This part had been the "no man's land" for two years. The Somme offensive commenced July 1st 1916. From that date, the Germans had been pushed steadily back. Shell holes. In the villages no two bricks were standing together. Still these French houses were very frail. We used to say that anyone could break into a French house with a good sized jack-knife. They did not take a deal of knocking down. A direct hit with a delayed action shell would do it. Vegetation was scarce, and the numerous graves told the tale.

We arrived at our destination at the position we were supposed to have taken over, but the enemy had retired. This position was not in range. The guns were parked in a sunken road 400 yards to the rear, and we took up our billets on the position. And it was some position. For months it had been the home of a French .75 battery. From the appearance, we came to the conclusion that the Frenchmen believed in comforts. The position was a fine example of workmanship.

Never did we again see such a position. Well with us, building material was scarce at times and we were lucky if we managed to get a sheet of roofing iron to keep off the rain. Now as to this position, the pits were built of wood and were well protected. A 10-foot deep trench ran at the rear of the pit with steps up to each gun. This trench was covered in so one could walk in safety from one end of the battery to the other. The dugouts were deep. Would take more than an eight inch to disturb them. The French lookout man it seemed had a little fortress all on his own. A telephone he had, and bells from his lookout to every dugout. It must have been a lovely war. Douglas and I claimed an old cookhouse as our billet. We had made a good inspection of the deep dugouts. Rats were too numerous. Did not fancy it. At night others too joined us— others also who did not care for the rats. We gathered in a good supply of wood for the fire - guess the French men would have cried to see their handiwork going up in smoke. Still the troops had to be kept warm.

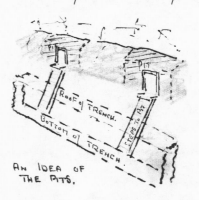

AN IDEA OF THE PITS.

In the evening, several of us had a stroll through Belloy Wood. (It had been a wood). Visited both the old British and German front line trenches. These had been occupied only a few days before. What a mess. Could hardly put a foot down without touching some implement of warfare. Bombs, yards of machine gun tape, hundreds of rifles, bayonets. Men we saw, many half buried. Three dead Germans we saw, in a shell-hole. Skin had gone black. We returned with a few relics. I had found a good sheepskin or goatskin coat. One of our party had found a skull with gold false teeth. He was of course, proud of them. I remember that for months he carried them round in his mess tin. I suppose that he removed them at mealtimes. I should hardly fancy seeing them floating in a mess tin of "bully" stew. Well at dusk we returned to our place of abode. I can remember well what a game we had with our fire. A huge fire we made. I do not know whether the chimney required sweeping or not, but the smoke at one time, we had to put on our gas helmets, and there we sat like a — well, it looked like a conference of Klu Klux Klan Officials. And when the smoke had cleared, the fire burned brightly. Was a case of sitting well back. Black as niggers we were — Hungry. That day we had no food, we lived in hopes of a meal coming, but no. We dropped off to sleep. Another day gone.

22nd March

Up at 8.30 a.m. Mistake in the time, this being
the first day of summer time (daylight saving
scheme). As to the summer time, well I do not
know. Snow fell nearly all day. At mid-day the
ration wagon came up. Guess we were thankful. A
good dinner we had. When the next, we did not
know. Snow fell nearly all day. We felt it. If one
has experienced being hungry on a cold day, well
they know what it means. We spent the day
scrounging in the dugouts. What finds we had.
We collected bundles of camouflage. This was
pieces of green and brown rag, tied onto wire
netting. We were much interested in a company
of the Bengal Lancers passing by. Fine big men
they were. Cigarettes ran out. Turned in at 5
p.m and we were soon asleep. Why the delay we
then wondered. We never knew anything and
were not supposed to know. We could only guess
and form our own opinions. The Germans had
retired and had made sure that they would not
be troubled until they were nicely dug in. They
destroyed every bridge over the Somme. The
bridge building on the part of our engineers was
carried out in day and night, but it meant a
delay. The Somme was not an extra wide river,
but it needed a good bridge for heavy transport.

23rd March

A quiet day. German planes up. First time we had seen. Was my luck to do a guard that night. Wet and cold "skipper" Clark and I did a 9-hour stretch. We walked up and down, Clark telling yarns and he could tell them. Nearly 60 perhaps and hard as nails. Been to sea on a trawler all his life. The "run" of one yarn I still remember; how one night his boat put into the docks at Yarmouth. I suppose that he had had a good fill of LACONS. (a former Yarmouth Brewery) When walking through the market place, he saw a woman in a sort of invalid chair. She passed some uncalled-for remark as he passed. He went back. This woman had no legs. I forgot to mention that he took off his belt. Passing his belt under her arms, he lifted her out of her chair and hung her on the church railings. Two hours after, when he passed, she was still hanging there. A specimen of his yarns. One needn't believe them. We didn't do badly. All that day we had had no food. But Skipper Clark had been on the lookout. Where he got the biscuits and tea from, I do not know. We had a good feed. These old soldiers are artful - (Or sailors in this case). A messenger came up from "A" Battery. I did my best to lead him to the Officers dugout, and a job it was too. A black night and the ground pitted with water filled shell holes. Although only perhaps 500 yards, we were nearly 3/4 hour getting there.

24th March

Pulled guns into line for moving off. Washed down.

25th March

Frost and snow. Only breakfast that day. Next meal was at 3 a.m next morning. Sure it was a good thing that there was practically no work. Suppose that it always took time for the supply columns to settle down when going out as a new division and then again there was the advance.

26th March

March 26

Battle of Gaza begins

Breakfast 3 a.m. Moved off at 4 a.m. A miserable morning, Being dark made it more dreary. Through Barleau to Eterpigney. Left guns by the side of the road. Horses were taken back. We had gone a good distance when Jack Wringe realised that he had left something on the gun. I walked back there, and I had forgotten to ask where I should find the wagon line. By the way, it was at Belloy. I wandered about all morning. Poured with rain and the state of the roads — well - still I happened lucky. I came across a clearing party. Burying the dead — they were partaking of refreshment. I told them the tale

and was invited to join them. On returning, I
would boast of having had a good feed. At the
same time they directed me to a canteen. I
managed to get a few packets of biscuits. This
pleased the remainder of the detachment.
Arrived at the wagon line. Found the other boys.
Playing cards down in a vault in the churchyard. I have heard of some queer things, but this
beats all. And this tomb was to be our sleeping
place that night. Not that it mattered to me,
but Wringe did not like the idea. He found quite
a good dugout. Meals we had regular. We had
our first rum and cigarette issue.

27th March

Up at 7 a.m. We had busy morning putting up
new horse-lines in the wood. (Well only the stumps
that were left). Snow again. We had a walk
round. Some rather unpleasant sights – walked 7
miles to small canteen belonging to the
Lincolnshire Infantry. We managed to get a few
cigarettes.

28th March

In the morning, we packed all our kit on the
"first line" wagon, and at noon we moved off.
The weather was now fairly good. I rode an "off"
horse again at the gun-park at Eterpigney.
Packed up gun. Commenced to rain. Again,

through shattered villages and we saw the
covering methods of the enemy. Trees were cut
down and placed across the roads, also telegraph
poles. (These had been removed by advance
parties). We noticed that every fruit tree in the
district had been cut down. At every crossroads
there was a huge mine crater. A hole that would
often cover a good-sized house. Roads had to be
made round these craters. We noticed that many
of the wells had either been filled in with rubbish
or poisoned. We arrived at BRIE. The bridge there
was not finished, so we had to go further down
the river to St CHRIST.

A MINE CRATER
AT A CROSS ROADS.

Pontoon bridge. Had to pass over one at a time.
(One gun or wagon at a time). Very few guns
could be heard. An occasional rumble on our left.
We halted a mile from bridge. Waited until
column was again made up before we moved on.
We wandered round, scrounged a supply of

firewood. (We were new at this scrounging business). We were what could be termed as "slow". In other words we did not know what belonged to us. Why everything belonged to us only for the trouble of taking. One fared badly if one did not agree to these methods.) Well at this particular time, we should have been more comfortable if we had not been such novices at the game — but by experience, we learned much. Anyway, during this halt we scrounged a good supply of firewood. We arrived at Cartigney. It was dark. Did not see much of the place, only that at the place where we halted there were the remains of a sugar refinery. This was the wagon line for the battery when we were in action until we moved to Hesbecourt. It then snowed hard. An awful night. We went forward 3 kilometres with the guns. Put guns in position. All was quiet, could hear firing on our left. The position was at back of small belt of trees on crest of hill. Until 11 p.m we were busy cutting down branches of trees, and "planting" them round gun to conceal them. Not a thankful job on such a night as that was. And we could not use a light. We then laid down in the snow under the gun limber. We were dead tired but too wet and cold to sleep. We were called out at 2 a.m. Something did not please the major. Had to clear the "line of fire" in wood.

29th March

3 a.m. Went down to the valley. One biscuit and jam and hot water. First for 24 hours. We dried our coats by a fire. Found a stable, turned in until 8 a.m. Felt much better. One biscuit and hot water. Our only meal that day. We straightened up. Looked much better. Order came to pack up. Moved to another position a mile or so in front. Again, in a wood. We pulled the guns in the wood so no camouflage was needed. Three of us had to stand by one gun. I was one. I do not think that in all my experiences did I ever have such a rough night with regards to the weather. Sure, there were rougher nights but we were prepared for them. Well it rained, poured the whole night. If I had fallen in a river, I could not have been wetter. As a rule, our overcoats kept out the rain, but it failed to do so on this particular night. I remember that it "leaked out" a week or so later that two of the detachment had a good supper and how they came by it – they would never say.

30th March

At 7 a.m the rain stopped. We made a great fire and dried our clothes. On this day, we saw our first air fight. Rather exciting we thought it, but it was only a mild one. A good dinner. Commenced to snow again. Thought that we were

in for another lively night. At 4 p.m we moved
forward. Passed through Boucly. Passed over fields
to right of Tincourt and Hamel. During this
journey, we heard the first drone of the shell.
They passed over and dropped over the hill
somewhere in the region of Roisel. Yes at last we
were within reach of his guns. At such a time,
one feels a trifle curious. Curious as to what a
shell burst looks like. Is there a terrific report
when at close quarters? etc. We arrived at our
destination Hamelet. We pulled guns by hand off
the road, up a bank and into a garden belonging
to houses at the side of the road (or what was
left of the houses). Still they were not as badly
smashed as some we had seen. A garden. It had
been a nice little garden once, I suppose. Fruit
trees etc. One learns by experience they say. Well
it was so in this garden. Still we could only smile
at the misfortunes that followed. We could fire a
gun, but we could not make a gun bed. The
ground was very soft. Even as we pulled guns, the
wheels sank some inches. We made a platform of
bricks and pulled the gun onto this platform.
Sure it looked well and we were pleased with
ourselves. A canopy of camouflage we placed over
the gun. Made a rack for our ammunition. At
11 p.m we had a meal and settled down in a
barn at the rear of the gun. Quite comfortable.
Straw on floor. Had been a German billet. We

listened for a while to the drone of German 4.2 and 5.9 shells that passed over us. A thud informed us that they had found a billet way back in Tincourt and Hamel and then we dropped off to sleep, forgetting everything. About the shells. It is hard to describe the noise that a shell makes in its flight. Various sounds. When months had passed we will know the different sounds. Some like a far off heavy luggage train – these would be heavy shells – a long range and would burst miles to the rear. Then would be the sound like someone walking along with a pair of loose fitting slippers. These too one could smile at. Then there was the shell that had a sort of whistle. These would be lighter shells, falling. Perhaps 400 yards to the rear – but if you heard a sort of sound that one hears when standing on a railway platform and an express rushes through. At such a sound no matter whether the shell was large or small, keep low!

31st March

Up at 8 a.m. A nice morning. Ordered to be ready at 10 a.m and at that hour we registered what a surprise we had. Three rounds only we fired. We must have been well under the enemy's observation. He too opened out. Shells burst 300 yards in front and gradually crept nearer. We were awfully curious to see the bursts. With

interest we gazed at them over our gun shields,
but in less than five minutes we knew enough
about shell bursts to last us for a few days. The
shells fell thick in the garden and back on the
road. A warm quarter of an hour. We had orders
to take cover. We lay down by the side of wall in
front of the gun. Wall was hit 2 yards to the left
of gun. Shed completely demolished 4 yards to the
rear. We were covered with bricks and dust. D sub
gun had two spokes knocked out of the wheel.
Sergeant Lingard was wounded. 3 infantrymen
killed on the road behind. We wondered if this
was a usual occurrence. If it was, our lives would
have been short. We realised that a gun shield
did not afford a deal of cover, so we started
digging a trench in the rear of the gun. At 1
p.m and lasting until 4 p.m we put up a
barrage. Also other batteries in the vicinity, and
we had no direct response to our fire. Shells passed
over but that that did not matter so long that
they did not disturb our garden. Drove Germans
out of Hervillers at range 3,500. After about 30
rounds, our gun bed gave way. Wheels had sunk
nearly a foot. We piled in more bricks, was
hopeless. We carried on. Major spotted the battery
that had shelled us. Called for 9 degree switch
from us, but we could not do it. But the other
batteries caught them. They had to move, and
moved in such a hurry that they left a gun

wagon behind, and two dead horses. We found them near the position that we went to next day. The infantry advanced.

OUR FIRST EXPERIENCE

We finished at 6,300 yards. We after the "straff" made new gun bed but did not use it. Out there one had always to prepare for the worst. If arriving at a position it was work all night. Making shelter might never have to use them but one never knew — we cleaned gun and got to bed at 7 p.m. After talking over the excitements of the day, we settled down to sleep.

1st April

Packed up. Had to move up — being practically out of range we had a quiet day. Received our first mail from England and it was our first pay-day in the line. Moved off at 7 p.m. A dark night it was. Through Hervillers. At this village we were delayed nearly two hours. The enemy had left it in rather a mess. Every moveable article

had been thrown over the road. Trees, barb wire
and mine craters. And the village was still
burning. With the help of the infantry, we made
a road through and at the same time, shells were
falling unpleasantly near. On to Hesbecourt. Was
a cold dark night. Could not see much as to what
the position was like. We pushed the guns into a
hedge and commenced digging a trench. Our
adventure at Hamelet had taught us the
necessity of making cover. So in the dark we dug.
No lights were allowed being only 2000 yards
from the enemy.

HERVILLEES APRIL 1st.

We worked hard. We did not know how soon the
cover might be needed. By 4 a.m we had a
trench to each gun about 5 foot deep and 18 foot
long. And at that, we packed up. Made a big
bed with all blankets and turned in. "Heads
under" to shut out the sounds of the shells
bursting in the village and then sleep.

April 2

US President Woodrow Wilson delivers war address to Congress

2nd April

Up at 8 a.m. A white frost, blankets were like boards, but we had been really comfortable. Did not fancy getting up. After breakfast we put up camouflage and improved on our trench and same time, digging deeper and made steps at end. Walked to wood on right to get tree branches and with these, continued the hedge at the side and rear of gun. With this and the camouflage the guns could not be seen when 25 yards away. All day we were busy then came night, and a miserable one too. Rain and snow. When fine one could put blankets down on the ground and all would be well. All night we walked about. Cursing our bad luck and making suggestions as to what we should do when daylight came. A shelter from the weather was needed. Shells dropped near. They helped to break the monotony.

3rd April

Did not feel extra bright after the sleepless night. We enlarged trench. Dug out ledge to serve as a seat. And from the village we obtained some wood. A door or two. With these, we made a roof. Village shelled heavily. Several killed and wounded in our D Battery. Heavy guns (60 pound[er]s) came up to Hervillers. Received "stand to". 1-4 Lincs (Lincolnshires) went into the line. Enemy then held the quarries which was quite a

stronghold. Poured with rain. Our shelter was not
much of a success. The roof leaked badly. But
that night, we did not get a chance to think of
sleep. Lincolnshire infantry advanced from open
ground. Had to retire with heavy losses. We fired
nearly all night and helped to bandage up the
infantry who crawled back.

4th April

Snow and rain. Douglas and I scavenged round.
We decided to find somewhere a dry resting-place
for the night if we managed to get time. In the
village, about three hundred yards from the guns
we found an old farm cart. This we turned
upside down. Dug down about a foot and there
was our billet. We were proud of it, and at the
same time we commenced widening one end of
our trench. Barrage at night. 5 Leicesters is
beaten back with deadly machine gun fire.

OUR BILLET AT HESBECOURT.

Heavy losses. We turned in at 2 a.m but disturbed 2 hours later to unload ammunition. At 5 a.m turned in again. Slept well until 8 a.m.

5th April

Snow. Slept all afternoon. We had a good rum issue in the morning. Perhaps that is why we slept so well. On duty at night. We sat in the trench. Made a fire in an old petrol tin. A fire was comforting. The enemy very active. Several shells dropped unpleasantly near. We passed the night hours away quite well. We had tea and plenty of rum. We told yarns, sung etc.

6th April

April 6

US declares war on Germany

Fired all morning. Right section were moved further to right so as to have a more direct "line of fire". In other words to clear the crest with lower elevation. The idea was to cut the barb wire. This was more effective with lower elevation.

Thus:

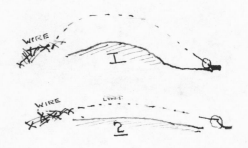

More damage done as in no. 2. We carried ammunition for these two guns. Making dugout at end of trench.

7th April

Snow again. Enemy very lively. Had just finished dinner, were sitting round brazier in building next to road. (4 walls covered with a trench sheet, this place was used as billet for D, E, & F gunners but was used as a sort of shelter for all) When with a shriek a shell burst in the doorway, and everyone sitting opposite to the door was either killed or wounded. Quite a shock to us.

Killed outright:

    Bombardier Miller (Grimsby)
    Gunner Bray (Hatfield)

Wounded:

    Bombardier Nightingale (Grimsby)
        He died the next day.
    Gunner Padmore (he died a week later)
    Gunner Paget (lost his hand)
    Jack Howard (lost his foot)
    Gunner Bloom, and several minor wounds.

We bandaged up the wounded. Nightingale's leg was blown nearly off, and he was still conscious. When in the stretcher, he said "goodbye boys, I guess it will be a --- organ job for me. When I get

out of hospital you will see me standing at
Freeman Street Corner". Jack Howard could not
believe he was wounded. Said his foot felt a bit
stiff. Only a small wound but he lost his foot. I
helped to carry him to "Aid Post". On return,
Douglas and I stitched Bray up in a blanket.
Bray was in our sub, so it was up to us. Cannon
was too upset. Bray and Cannon were real pals,
and the same with Miller, he also had a brother
in the battery. Was hard luck to see his brother
killed. Later we went grave digging in the
cemetery. Jack Inman, Douglas and myself. Not
a job that I liked. At night, Bombardier Starling
came up in Bray's place. A sad crowd we were
and Starling's arrival did not cheer us up. He
was upset because that day he had been reduced
from sergeant to bombardier. Until that day we
had had but little to do with him. He was a
brainy fellow and old Territorial, but no go in
him. Absent minded we found him. Jack Wringe
thought a lot of him. But it seems as though he
had upset one of the heads of the battery and so
was reduced. Wringe told us about it and how it
had affected him. Wringe asked us to treat him
well. We found him one of the best. In a week or
so he told us that he was far happier than when
he had his stripes. Other detachments used to
tease him. That we never did. It was a lively
night. One shell just missed our dugout. (We had

then transferred ourselves from the cart to the newly made dugout in the trench.)

8th April, Easter Sunday

Fired all morning. Six of us went up as burial party. The divisional Chaplain performed the service. Covered in, and on top planted some flowering plants. Marking graves with wood from ammunition box until cross could be made. Snow again. An easy afternoon. In the cemetery was a huge cross, erected to two English airmen who were killed there or near there. The aeroplane propeller was fixed on the cross.

This cross had been erected by the Germans.

HESBiCOURT.

9th April

Shell carrying for the right section. Again they were wire-cutting. Snow again.

April 9 - 20

Nivelle Offensive (Second Battle of Aisne, Third Battle of Champagne) ends in French failure

April 9

Canadian success at the Battle of Vimy Ridge

10th April

Snow. Never have I known such a stretch of wintry weather. We had an easy day. Jock had a toothache. He took a liberal dose of rum, and the others helped him. Perhaps it was well that it was an easy day. Jock and his swinging bottle. He had always a full bottle of rum hanging above his head when he went to sleep. Said that it roused him up no end when it came into collision with his head in the mornings. And I believe it. At night, we took over "B" sub dugout for guard. Why I do not know. No sleep. Made up a good fire and on the whole quite enjoyed ourselves.

11th April

I note by the original that this day was a Wednesday. But what did the day matter whether Sunday or weekday it didn't make any difference.

12th April

Straightening up

A few more descriptions of the position and surroundings. As I described before, the guns were in a hedge bank. A long garden with a few fruit trees in front, and the in front of that another hedge. Length of position about 400 yards. Although so short a distance, we seemed to move about only in a little area between dugout and gun except to give a pull now and again, if a gun had run off its platform etc. In the first place there was always plenty of work and again, we always had to be on the spot and ready for action. Of course, the Battery always met at mealtimes but really with other detachments we did not mix. Well - not to any extent. If we wanted help, we used to call in our partner detachment "F" sub. But for certain reasons, we preferred to be independent if possible. On our left was the road from Hervillers to---? The road must have cut through the quarries in front, but where I did not know. At the opposite side of the road was what had been a farm house and buildings. These – (or in this farm yard) were the Officers dugout, cook house, signallers headquarters, Battery Office etc. Then at right angles was the Village street with a huge crucifix at the junction of the roads. From the heaps of bricks and rubbish one could hardly imagine as to what sort of village it had been. Half way through the village was the well and it

was the only well that could be used for some
miles around. And the "buckets" were old biscuit
tins, so water drawing was not a thankful
occupation. And this water had to be – what
shall I say – made drinkable. When adulterated
with chloride of lime water was not very inviting
even in the hottest weather. Even the tea we had
tasted strongly of chloride. Suppose it had to be so.
At the top end of the village was a dressing
station. Another dressing station was situated in
front of guns. To rear of guns, back to Hervillers
was a sort of heath, and to the right was "BOIS"
wood. Well that is an idea as to what our
surroundings were like. Now as to the
detachments. In the gunnery books one reads "a
gun detachment consists of ten men". Well it
really consisted of as many available men possible.
At this position the battery was well represented.
There were times later when the strength would
diminish down to two men and no reserves. But
we were kept at full strength here. This was our
detachment.

11th and 12th April

Easy days

13th April

A nice day. Improving our dugout. At 6 p.m we
went up with F sub. To Bois Wood quite in the

open. We prepared a pit, filled a few sandbags.
At 9 p.m, prepare position for a lone gun. This
position being on the left front of Bois Wood. A
wagon in charge of Sergeant Coppin came up
with ammunition. This was unloaded and stored
away in the "dumps" that we had roughly
constructed, and at 10 p.m we started back for
the position. Was easy enough to find ones
bearings in the daytime but a far different
matter it was at night. It was a beautiful
starlight night and quiet. Hardly a shot being
fired. Not a single light from the trenches, really
peaceful. We could have walked back to the
Battery but with chance of a ride, we accepted
it. About 6 of us gunners were seated in the
bottom of a general service wagon, talking etc.
Not noticing where we were going. Time went on
but still we did not arrive at our destination
and then Coppin confessed that he was lost. I
remember our old friend Sammy Starling was
trying to find his whereabouts by the stars. And
Coppin heard a few perhaps uncomplimentary
remarks. On we went. Believe me, it was none too
thrilling an experience, a sort of deathlike silence
on the Front, and we were aimlessly wandering
about not many hundred yards from the
trenches with six horses and wagon too. Wouldn't
the enemy have been pleased. At last we arrived
at a village. Houses still burning and at the end

of the village we were challenged by a solitary outpost. "Where the ---- have you come from"? he asked. Templeau this village was. The enemy had only abandoned it that morning. The outpost said: "Consider yourselves -----lucky" and we did. We arrived back at the battery at 2 a.m and vowed never more to trust the guidance of Coppin.

14th April

Finished dugout

15th April

Heavies came up to Hesbecourt . 60 pounders. Their position was just at the left of the cemetery. Preparing for big barrage. Zero hour was 12.15 a.m. Infantry went over, Villnet (Villeret) was captured. S.O.S at 4.30. Enemy was driven off and on left.

16th April

Perbeek Farm was captured and we stood by all day. Firing at intervals. Cleaning up. Captive balloon came up to Hervillers. Only been up half an hour when it was attacked by a German plane. The balloon was no more.

17th April

Snow again, up all night. Firing every few minutes and a barrage at 6 a.m.

April 16

*Lenin arrives in Russia
Second battle of the Aisne begins*

April 17

French tanks used for the first time in battle

18th April

Easy day. Digging Observation Point in No Mans Land. Indians in the line. Went up as fatigue with ----(?). Two infantrymen accompanied us one having a Lewis gun. A dark night. When nearing front line trench we were "pulled up" by a Hindoo. He would not let us pass. All we could get out of him was "Password". We had heard nothing about passwords. They escorted us to a "sap" (deep dugout). Was a comfortable spot, could hardly imagine that such a place could exist only a few yards from the front line. Our captors could not speak English. They seemed not to heed us. They squatted down in a far corner. After some time we thought it best to enlighten them as to our mission. We asked for the officer. One of them condescended to tell the officer. And the verbal message that came back would shock the reader. Still we were allowed to go on our way. We were conducted to a pathway through the barbed wire and crawled along to the Observation Point. Fairly quiet except from an occasional livener from a machine gun.

This Observation Post was the cellar of a ruined house. We had just to clear out the loose bricks and rubbish and reinforce the doorway with sandbags. Not a bad nights work. Our light was only a shuttered siege lamp. Just a faint glow.

At 4 a.m we started again for the battery arriving at daybreak.

19th April

Ammunition, making new dumps. Barrage.

29th April

April 29 - May 20

Mutiny breaks out among French army

Between the two dates, nothing of importance happened. Just the daily routine. Occasional shots during the day and night shoots. On this day we put up a big barrage on <u>Cologne Farm</u> and the chalk pit or quarry. By the number of shells that fell in this quarry, one would imagine that there would be little of it left. The Lincolnshires were in the line and they this day lost nearly half a battalion. Such heavy machine gun fire. Until dinner time we kept up a continuous fire. Then it quietened down. A nice day — in the evening, Doug and I were detailed for baths at <u>Roisel</u>, six kilometres to left rear. The outing we much enjoyed.

BATHS AT ROISEL.
(SOMME)

Roisel had been quite a nice little country town.
It had been. At this time, a heap of bricks. Still
to such a place as this it was nice to get back to.
The streets were free of rubbish. No doubt much
more tidy than in its pre-war state. The roads
had been renamed. And many of the names were
familiar, such as Regent Street, Manchester
Road, etc. A band was playing near the station.
(Notts. and Derby Band). We visited the B.E.F.
(British Expeditionary Force) canteen getting a
supply for ourselves and others of the battery. And
at 9 p.m we started on our homeward journey.

30th April

A quiet day. At night it was my turn for S.O.S
Guard on hill near Brigade HQ. This was to look
out for S.O.S rockets in case that the telephones
were put out of action. These rockets were fired
from an ordinary rifle – bursting into a series of
coloured lights, perhaps a red and two greens -
these signals were changed every few days. The
guard on duty also had a rocket. On seeing the
signal from the trenches, he would fire his to
warn the guns further back and so all along the
line and the response to the signals commenced in
a very few seconds.

6th May

Went up to reserve position in front of <u>Bois</u> <u>Wood</u>, as guard. No gun there, only ammunition. Not a very pleasant job, being on one's own. I remember making up my bed on top of shells, and remembered no more until morning. Still it was rather a bad principle to send a lone guard. If anything had happened, well - on my way back, I found a dead Indian. He had been wounded. He had unwound his turban for a bandage — yards of it.

7th May

A captive balloon broke loose and floated very low over our position. Some guns in rear tried to hit it, but no, it drifted over the enemy's line.

And so we carried on. Weather now was quite good and we were not hard worked and the front became quieter. We had comfortable dugouts, food was good. In the evening we amused ourselves with different ball games etc. A gramophone playing and sing songs etc. The air forces were active on both sides. Air fights were plentiful. Really we were somewhat disappointed if we did not see our every evening air fight. Just as the sun was setting, a German flight would come over. This was met by our airmen and the conflict was always thrilling. Planes would fall in flames. Whether ours or theirs a cheer always went up from the batteries around.

Well until 15th May the daily routine was much of a sameness. On that day we heard that two guns were to be taken back to training school for officers behind the line. The officers drew lots and Lieutenant Alcombe won. The left section were to have a holiday

15th May

We were awfully pleased with ourselves. That night I went down to wagon line with Allen (F Gun) to make preparations. Rode in cook's cart. Roisel. Kits fell off when crossing stream near Roisel. Was dark when we arrived at wagon line. We scrounged a supper from the wagon line cook George Inkson (an old friend of mine).

16th May

Painting, first line and firing battery wagons. The wagon line was known as Happy Valley – and I guess it was. The drivers were having a good time and had comfortable billets. Some in tents, some in cave like dwellings in the banks. At night Allen and I went to Roisel. Half hour walk perhaps. Went to the canteen and had to scramble under cover. The town was shelled with eight inch shells. A lot of damage done – several killed.

May 12 - October 24
10th, 11th and 12th Battles of Isonzo fought, ending in Italian failure

May 15 - 16
Petain becomes French Western Front Commander in Chief

May 19

John Pershing given command of American Expeditionary Force

17th, 18th and 19th May

We were busy painting.

20th May

Finished painting wagons. Heavy thunderstorm. Happy Valley flooded.

21st May

The guns and detachments came down that night. We made a "bivi" with a trench sheet thrown over gun. Really it was nice to know that undisturbed could continue sleeping until the morning.

OUR BIVI AT HAPPY VALLEY.

22nd May

Loaded up with shells. Baths. Walk over the fields to Y.M.C.A. at Tincourt. Piano and singsong. Yes we had a most enjoyable evening.

23rd May

Reveille at 4.30. Moved off at 9 a.m to where we did not know. We only knew that we were bound

for a sort of land of peace. That was enough.
When at the end of the valley, the wheel of the
gun went over my foot. Nothing serious as luck
happened. Through <u>Tincourt</u>. Saw Abery
(Melbourn). Had a few words with him. We
halted at <u>Duingt</u> for dinner. The surroundings
were far different to when we first came up.
Huge dumps, camps and railway sidings had
sprung up. Y.M.C.A. at D(oingt). Through
Peronne. This had been a big town and it was
not too badly damaged. Watered horses in the
Somme. At the same time we gunners went to
the canteen B.E.F. Through Estrees. Past the old
position to Proyart - Now a nice little village.
Civilians had returned. We made a "bivi" over
the gun, found a nice little estaminet and spent
a very pleasant evening.

24th May

Cleaning up. Walk around with a Signal Corps
Sergeant Major. Slept again in "bivi".

25th May

Reveille at 5.30 a.m Packed up. This packing up
took time. Bits had to be tidily packed. Corn and
hay had to be tied onto wagons. Moved off 9 a.m
through <u>Hamel</u>. Not a sign of war now. A very
hot day. Passed through <u>Amiens</u>. Halted at
Y.M.C.A. We wondered how much further we were

going. Amiens we wished to see more of. At last we were at our destination Vaux. Pulled into sheds.

26th May

A hot day. Washed down. I will describe the place. This was a school for Officers. I never knew what officers they would be, but should imagine that they were men who had just taken commissions in the Artillery. Anyway, they were quite new to the game. Our guns they used for drill. And with our horses they had riding instruction. I had two to help, one in the gun park. Everything had to be clean, and everything ready for their use. Was easy for us. We used to rush round in the morning before their parade. So between the hours 9 a.m and 12, and 2 p.m to 4.30 we had nothing to do. These officers were put through it. They had six months training pushed in four weeks. And were kept at it. It amused us to see them. We limber gunners made a holiday of it. The weather was ideal. Back of the gun shed was a nice shady tree and if we were required – well, they knew where to find us. A little estaminet stood near by. Beer we could buy at about two pence a quart bottle. What a time. The other gunners and drivers did well but of course they had the daily task of grooming – and we limber gunners too were exempt from guards at night.

(Jack Wringe's doings I guess) Vaux was a nice
little village and the country round was very
much like the average English countryside, and
being in late May, it looked at its best. The
population of Vaux was perhaps 500. We were
billeted in a barn belonging to a farm. Quite
comfortable. Wire beds built in tiers 3 high. Down
the road was the cook house and adjoining that a
recreation room. As to food, we did well. We
always bought eggs for breakfast. Being hot
weather, we seldom tackled the stew. It was
greasy stuff in hot weather so more rice was
prepared and milk we used to buy at the farm
house.

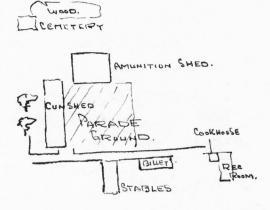

26th May

Long walks we used to make. Sometimes 16 miles
during the evening. Many passed whole night
playing cards, and many a night we preferred
sleeping out rather than in the barn. Anyway

not so many "livestock". And so the days went by. Nothing very exciting happened. Here are the "Doings" as entered in the Diary plus a few extra remarks.

27th May

Gun inspection, a busy day.

28th May

Washing wagons.

May 28

Pershing leaves New York for France

29th May

Sorting amo. Café in village at night.

3rd June

Inspection. Afternoon; walk into <u>Allis</u> <u>sur</u> <u>Somme</u>. A pretty village. Tea at Café. Had quite a good time – were much amused by a man driving cows. Here he walked in front of the herd blowing a horn and the animals following him. This horn blowing stunt seemed quite a craze. Every dinner-time, a funny little fellow (he seemed all trousers) came to Vaux on a bicycle selling copies of the "Continental Daily Mail". Blowing his horn to warn us of his

THE NEWSPAPER SELLER

approach, He always visited us in the gun sleds.
What a game we used to have with him. Still
every day he came. We would tie him to the gun,
exercise his cycle taking no notice of his yells. In
spite of this treatment, he always visited us
every day.

4th June

Painting again. Another two guns arrived on the
same stunt as ourselves. From the 181 Bat. 40
Division. An East End crowd and a lively one too.
These were 4.5 guns. With them were Sergeants
Mully and Jolly. Mully took over charge of the
gun shed.

7th June

Terrific thunderstorm. Village street was flooded
to a depth of three feet, much to the delight of
the village boys.

June 7
*The British Army
explodes 19 large
mines under the
Messines Ridge*

8th June

A day in Amiens — and it was a day too. The
City then had not been shelled. We visited most
of the principal sights, the Cathedral, etc. Went
to a Market. Have never before or since seen so
many eggs. Cafes we visited, (a change for us).
All roads into Amiens were well guarded. But for
future visits we noted how these sentries could be
dodged.

9th June

Packed up at 10 a.m. Walked to <u>Poulingville</u> (Poulainville) with Douglas and Inman. Quite a day in the country. Took our rations for dinner. Inman collecting blackthorn for making walking sticks. He was quite clever at this game. At a café at Poulingville we had a good time. Piano and sing-song. Finished up at cinema at Army Service Corps camp.

Sunday, 10th June.

Morning: We picked the lock of the ammunition store, getting up at 3 a.m for this exploit. Filled our haversacks with Mills bombs. At 10 a.m three of us went on a fishing expedition. Walked to <u>Allis-sur-somme</u>. We had already seen a boat anchored up the river. Believe me there wasn't much that escaped us. This boat we borrowed (without asking of course). We thought that if we tried to explain to the owner that we wished to borrow it, he wouldn't understand or he wouldn't wish to. To save trouble we did not ask. Down stream we went, and commenced our fishing. The method I will explain. A Mills bomb is an egg shaped affair. A split pin is withdrawn. This releases the lever, which springs up and strikes the detonator when leaving the hand.. A few seconds later, the bomb bursts. Well these we threw into the water. Throwing them and falling down in the boat so as not to stop a stray piece of metal – a bang and a spurt of water, and we rowed back to collect the dead fish that floated to the surface of the water. Yes it was a profitable trip. We returned to Vaux at 7 p.m, bought a loaf of bread and made a good supper.

11th June

Walked to Bertangles. In an estaminet we pulled on with a French soldier. He spoke English. Was home to help with the hay-making. We went to his house, a small farm, sampled his wine, and promised next evening to give him a hand in his hayfield.

13th June

At 4 p.m Doug and I started off to Bertangles. Inman followed later. We quite enjoyed ourselves hay making, supper at the farm. Our Frenchman returned to line next day.

14th June

In evening, walk to Fleselles returning via Fremont. Plenty of wild cherries and strawberries in the wood at Fleselles. Nearly as large as the cultivated fruit here.

15th June

June 15
US Espionage Act passed

Another visit to Amiens, this time without a pass. With a bit of scheming we passed the sentries over fences and back gardens. We went to the swimming bath and had quite a game with the Frenchmen. Hired a boat on the river. Shopping. Took tram back to Monterries. (Montiers) Squared the French sentries with tobacco and walked back to Vaux via Allis sur Somme. During the walk, we raided a cherry tree in a garden. The owner spotted us. The Language he used. Well we didn't understand him. We told him his cherries were "tres bien" but he didn't seem to appreciate the compliment.

16th June

A busy day. Giving demonstrations to classes of officers. Taking the buffers down etc, breach mechanism etc. Several of them wishing for further knowledge, asked me if they could take it down themselves after the class. This they did, although it was a Sunday. The tips received made it worth the trouble. The detachment always thankfully received such "windfalls".

17th June

Loaded up with ammunition and at 4 p.m left for a position just outside Vignacourt.. The officers were to have a firing course the following day. So Doug and I on "E" Gun, and Allen and Morris ("F" Gun) went to prepare and to look after guns. Took with us a Trench Sheet and a plentiful supply of rations. On arriving we were caught in a thunderstorm. Not very cheerful. The sheet we threw over the gun. In the evening, we walked into the village. Vignacourt was a fair sized village, and from all accounts had seen but few British Troops. We found a little place where "Madam" spoke English, and we were quite at home. After a supper, we returned to the guns. We had left them alone for five or six hours, still they were not articles that one would "pinch". Rather an uncomfortable night. Everything very wet.

18th June

Up at 4 a.m. Cleaned bores of guns. The officers arrived and started their firing at 6 a.m. We turned into bed again after breakfast and slept until 12 noon. Packed up and returned to Vaux at 2 p.m. Washed down.

19th June

A hot day. Thunderstorm in the morning. Warned for another expedition. Left for a position to right of Vignacourt, a much better spot. A wood of laburnum trees in rear – these trees were in flower. Just a mass of yellow. Our trench sheet

we tied on the trees, marking a good shelter.
Morris on these stunts acted as our cook – a
lively fellow – a fellow with a huge imagination.
Commenced to rain again so we turned in early.

20th June

Again, up at 4 a.m. Home at dinner time.
Cleaning down.

21st June

On fire picquet. Walk to wood for cherries. Visited
cemetery. Graves of quite a number of trench
mortar gunners who had been killed accidentally
at the school.

23rd June

Amiens in the afternoon. On the way home, we
met man who frequented our billets, exchanging
postcards for tins of bully. We stopped him. He
was loaded with bully. He thinking that we were
the police became nervous. We rolled him in the
grass. Thirty two tins - We took a postcard for
every tin he had.

24th June

Walk through Fremont to Vignacourt. Visiting
our friends of the 17th.

25th and 26th June

Guns were out all day on a sort of field day. We

June 26

*First US troops
arrive in France,
1st Division*

stayed behind. An easy time.

27th June

Four of us walked to Bertangles & Coisey. In the latter village, we found a dog. Of course, finding was keeping.

28th June

Thunderstorm. The officers held a boxing contest. Good sport.

29th June

Concert in the mortar school.

30th June

Started out for Amiens. Had to return owing to rain.

1st July

Walked via Madeline to Amiens. Canal Bank – stayed at café at Madeline on way home. You can quite imagine that we were having a good time. We hardly realised that there was a war on. We knew nothing of what was happening in the line, and I might add we did not care. The only reminder was the distant thunder of the guns and far off flashes could be seen at night.

8th July

Filled up with ammunition.

June 27

Greece enters the war on the side of the Allies

July 2

Pershing makes first request for army of 1,000,000 men

July 4

Air raid on Harwich

July 6

T. E. Lawrence and the Arabs capture Aquaba

July 7

Daylight Gotha raid on London, killing 57 civilians

9th July

Up to Vignacourt position again. Walked into village. Rain – tea and supper at our usual café. As usual, returning with a supply of eggs for breakfast.

Tuesday, 10th July

Same routine as before. Home at dinner time.

July 11

Pershing revises army request figures upwards to 3,000,000

11th July

Filled up, and at 4.30 up to the position by Fleselles. Went into village. A grand night. Did not even put up trench sheet.

12th July

Trouble with buffer. Returned. Spent afternoon repairing.

14th July

Warned for moving into the line again. Our holiday was drawing to a close.

15th July

Packing up

July 16

Third Battle of Ypres (Passchendaele) begins

16th July

Packing. Filling up with ammunition. Final inspection. Farewell concert in the messroom. And that ended it.

17th July

Up at 4 a.m. Moved off at 8 a.m. Not a very bright day and we were not feeling any too cheerful. Through Bertangles, Coisey, Villers, Bocage, to Vaux sur Somme. Our last night for a while in civilisation, and believe me, we celebrated it. Guns were parked in the Village street. We took up our quarters on the village green. A lovely evening, thought it would remain so, so did not trouble to erect our sheet. Jack Wringe started us off, and what happened, none of our detachment remembers. I know that I woke up finding that it was raining hard. Moved over to the church porch. Unable to find the other four.

18th July

Rain. We started off early. As to artillery on the march. People have the idea that it was quite a pleasure for a gunner when on the road. Riding all the while — well it was not so. Not in the 59th Division. The horses were not to be "overworked". It was seldom that a gunner was allowed to ride. It was our lot to plod along behind the gun or wagon as the case might be. Sometimes the column would be moving at a "dead march" pace, at other times at a trot or nearly so. This irregular pace is far more tiring than a straight forward march. Still no need to

July 17
King George V changes his name to Windsor

relate that we many a time perched ourselves on the gun trail. This being, when the "coast was clear". And at times we would get a changeover with a driver. Some of the drivers were not on the best of terms with the gunners. Why the difference, I do not know. They were not all the same though - still I know that some would stick in the saddle all day without giving a change over to a gunner. Summer time, of course — I have known the same driver begging a gunner to take his horses on a raw cold winters day. Quite a change then. Then the gunners would repay them, remind them of the hot summer days when they refused a ride etc. Of course, at night when going into action, we used to ride, being too dark to be seen. We always used the phrase "what we are supposed to do and what we do, are two different things." One would have fared rather rough if one did not take things that way. Returning to the journey. Commenced to rain and we arrived at the old Somme battle area Suzanne, Combles, Delville Wood on our right, and arrived at Combles. What a wilderness. Now the heaps of bricks and rubbish were overgrown with grass and weeds and the numerous graves were lost to view. We were still in the company of the 181 Brigade guns, and were billeted together in some huts near the church at Curlu. As to the church, only one wall was standing. On this wall

BRINGING IN GERMAN PRISONERS.

hung a huge crucifix quite undamaged. We
scrounged round, saw some tempting looking
currants on the other side of the stream. Made a
raft and crossed over. We collected from the huts
various useful articles, oilsheets, cooking utensils
etc., We turned in early.

19th July

We bid good-bye to our friends of the 181, and
started off again. On through Peronne to wagon
line in Happy Valley. Quite a welcome from the
battery. We learnt all the news of what had
happened in our absence. How that they now had
a new position etc., and we related about our
holiday and at the wagon line they had been
busy. A huge French hut had been erected. In
this hut, we slept that night.

20th July

We cleaned up, packed up our tools and at 8.30
p.m we started for the line. Though Roisel.
Position was at Templeau. Pits for our two guns
had been prepared, and with the help of the
remainder of Battery, we hauled the guns up the
bank into the pits. Was too dark to see what the
position was like. Doug and I were on S.O.S Guard.
A nice summer night – we wandered up and
down. Was light early, and we to pass the time,
started on a trench. The two of us worked until
breakfast time.

21st July

As to the position, it was fine. The whole six guns
were in a garden on the south side of village just
off the main road. Ten yards between each gun.
They had prepared quite a good pit for the gun
with sand-bag walls. Hardly "a pit". The gun
stood on top of ground, with a wall round, and
earthed up outside. We had been provided with
new camouflage. This was a string netting,
covered with pieces of coloured sack. The whole,
perhaps 30 feet square. At rear of gun was a
dense sort of undergrowth and in a sunken lane
in rear were the dugouts. Been prepared by the
infantry. Made of elephant iron. Comfortable
and safe.

POSITION AT TEMPLEUX.

In centre of battery was an underground dump holding perhaps 2,000 rounds of ammunition, all neatly packed.

22nd – 23rd July

Apart from trench digging and making new shell racks in our pit, we spent an easy day. Village was heavily shelled. What the village was like I do not know. I never did go into the village itself. Officer's dugout was to left of guns in a sort of courtyard and cookhouse was near main road.

24th July

6" Howitzer Battery on our right were straffed heavily with 8" shells. Dumps blown up. Shooting all night.

25th July

Work in pit.

26th July

Ranging. We now had about 30 different targets - ammunition up.

27th July

A day of air fights. Cutting branches in wood at rear to hide our guns. In wood we found some pumpkin plants. Brought some back. Much as we could carry. We were reported for using insulting remarks to officers and men of an aircraft section that stood just behind our dugout. These two guns we mounted on a lorry. The(y) would drive up and open up for action. A hostile aircraft would be sighted and they would fire on it. The machine they would never hit. (I never did see one hit by an "anti" gun.) The machine would return reporting the aircraft battery, and over would come the shells and at the first shell

AN "ANTI" AIRCRAFT GUN.

they would pack up and drive off and would be hours before we saw them again. We had the

shelling that was meant for them. So it was a
usual joke with us. We would call out in a loud
voice: "A shell, sir" "Where?" "A mile away, sir"
"PACK UP". Our officers laughed. Anyway, the
"anti" guns took up their positions further to the
left. Still we hadn't finished with them. When by
us we noticed that they had a petrol dump. This
dump was in the ground, and well hidden by
bushes. And we knew that they would have a like
dump at their new position. Two of us went to
investigate. One afternoon, we watched them
carefully concealing their dump. At night we
opened it out. Took six cans of petrol and replaced
same with cans of water. It was their reserve
supply. I wonder if they really did have to use it
- and I wonder what the result was.

DUGOUT AT TEMPLEAU.

Petrol was ideal stuff for clothes washing, and
was handy for cleaning the gun. On another
day, we watched the hiding of some barrows

belonging to a party of Royal Engineers who were laying a light railway on our left. At night, another raid. six barrows. Very handy too. Really, nothing was safe.

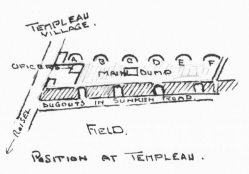

POSITION AT TEMPLEAU.

29th July

Relieved for a day at <u>Peronne</u>. One might think it strange going for a days outing, to a battered town such as Peronne. Still it was a change. Plenty of canteens, YMCA huts etc. One could always find amusement. Back up the line at night.

30th July

July 31

Major British offensive launched at Ypres

For some time, our gun had been far from running well. sent in report to Artificer scott (Brigade sergeant Fitter) He came back to test it. On duty at night.

Wednesday, 1st August

August 1

St. Julien Frezenburg, Pilken and Westhock were captured. Sanctuary Wood was attacked by the Australians and Hooge fell after heavy fighting

A heavy rain. The dugout used by those on duty fell in and "D". sub. dump collapsed. A busy day. By night, all was in order again.

2nd August

An easy day, Rain.

3rd August

Fired all day.

5th August

S.O.S at 2.30 a.m, and again at 4 a.m. several shells burst in our garden. Too near to be pleasant. In the morning the Inspector of Ordnance and Munitions inspected the guns and my gun was ordered to go to the repair shop. Packed up. Teams came up. Arrived at wagon line at 10 P.M. slept in Tent.

6th August

Slept in until 10a.m at dinner time. The battery fitter (Tiffy Mackay) and I left with gun for the ordnance workshop. Through Hamelet and Marquay to Hamel. The workshop had only the day before moved to this village. We spent the day helping to put things straight. Billet in a house. Not much damaged. Wire beds. We were quite comfortable and food was much better than at the battery. Rained at night. Spent evening at Church Army Hut. On leaving battery, we received "the unconsumed portion of the days ration and the rations for the next day". This was always the order. These we had to cook at new quarters and to receive the same quantity when returning. I always took the rations, but never handed them in. Of course receiving nothing when returning. Best of having a friend in the battery cookhouse. Always did well with George Inkson. With these rations we could provide ourselves with a supper each night. Mackay was a good fellow to go out with. A Scotchman of course.

7th August

Started at 7.30 a.m. Took down gun and buffers, and that day we did little else. Found a canteen in the next village. Went to the cinema at night. What a change since we were first in the district. Little hut towns had sprung up. Cinema, concert rooms etc., and quite good roads.

8th August

Started on our gun. Relining gunslides. This was done by brazing in strips of brass and then planing down to the required measurements. A slow job. Still it would have pleased us had it been slower. At night we went to a concert in the C.A hut.

9th August

On gun again. Fitted buffer with a tank. A new invention. Always sure of having enough oil in buffer with this tank. In evening, we walked to Y.M.C.A. at <u>Tincourt</u>. Met some of our "A" Battery friends.

10th August

In the evening walked with Tiffy across fields to wagon line. We had heard that they were having a pay day. This we did not want to miss. We called on our return to the old Hamelet position (where we fired our first shell). Was dark crossing the field, Tiffy fell into a shell hole. An uncalled for bath. Of course in spite of the language I could only laugh.

11th August

Gun ready. Left for wagon line. Call at Y.M.C.A. at <u>Marquay</u> and at 8 p.m left for the line. In the meantime, the battery had moved forward.

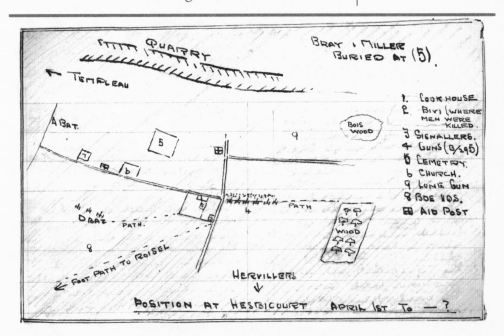

Position was now on the edge of the quarry. The remainder of battery had been busy.

TRENCH DIGGING

Had prepared a rough pit for our gun. Had erected the camouflage. I had a surprise for the detachment. On leaving Hamel had picked two sandbags of greengages. Plentiful they were that year. We had a good nights rest.

12th August

The position was very open. Guns in a line on side of hill, sloping up to brink of quarry (which was) 30 yards in front. This quarry was about 2 miles in length. 1/2 mile to left was road into Templeau. Should imagine that this position was in front (or east) of Hesbecourt. On our right was an old sugar refinery very much battered. A mass of twisted iron work and bricks. Quite a good dugout we had. This being an old cellar on the site of the factory. Steps leading down to it. And on top we piled bricks to stop a fair sized shell. At night the "Tynesides" attacked. Zero hour was 2 a.m. As they went over the guns opened out the Germans sent up a whole host of rockets. The whole front was lighted up. It was really a fine sight. Perhaps we noticed it more because we were high up and at the same time very near the line. Several S.O.S calls during the night.

13th August

Making main dump. Shells dropped in rear. Ten loads of ammunition. All had to be separated. More shelling. Was getting lively.

14th August

Sorting ammunition.

Various shells:
  Shrapnel 80 fuse
  Shrapnel 85 fuse
  High explosive delay
  High explosive none delay
Later we had the shell with the 106 fuse.
  Smoke shell
  Gas shells.

Later we had a stroll down to the quarry. Dugouts all along the banks. We were much surprised we had poured shells into this quarry when it was in German occupation. Not a sign of the damage done. In these quarry dugouts were billeted the Cambridgeshire and Suffolks waiting to relieve the Tynesiders that were then in the line. Met Charlie Gray of Royston and two Jarmans from Morden. We climbed up the opposite cliff. Were curious to see what was at the other side. Could look down on the enemy lines.

SHOWING USE OF CAMOFLAGE.

We had to be careful as crest was under observation. Returned to guns.

15th August

SOS GUARD AT THE QUARRY.

Cleaning shells. Rain at night. On our left we could see St Quentin burning. On S.O.S guard. This front is getting livelier every day. Expecting attack. Two men had to remain with gun day and night. Rumours of spies. Warned to be on the lookout for them. Shelled at night always and arguing as to who should go (up to the) observation post in the morning. Rather interesting. Both drunk. From what I could gather, the Major had been "telling them off". This was at 3 a.m.

16th August

"E" sub. went to prepare new position on right. I stayed with gun. Shelled heavy. I remember that I kept low. Remember with pride showing Doug and the others the lumps of shrapnel sticking in our sandbag wall. What they had missed. S.O.S while they were away. Had to get help. Shoot all night.

18th August

At 4 a.m. we were still at it. A beautiful sunrise and we had a(n) hours excitement. Twenty planes in single file machine gunned and bombed the trenches. So plain and yet unreal they seemed against the red sky. The Germans opened out with machine guns but no planes were hit. Preparing for a big barrage.

Sunday, 19th August.

"Better the Day"- Barrage commenced at 4 a.m. Covered advance with smoke. Fired until 8 A.M. Planes also supported the attack. Tyneside scottish in the line. Gillemont Farm captured. We had S.O.S all day. The Germans launched their big counter offensive. Jocks still held on. Suppose they had heavy losses.

20th August

Stood by all night, taking turns to sleep. 2 a.m. battery was shelled heavy. We retired to our trench. S.O.S 4 a.m, 3 p.m, 6 and 8.30 p.m. When firing during the afternoon, the flash from F gun set the dry grass alight. The camouflage on our gun and F gun was destroyed, and our guns stood in a bare black spot. We managed to stop it spreading further. A warm job. At 10 p.m we packed up. The teams arrived. Moved on (left section only) to a new position in the valley. Put up camouflage. Both guns wheel to wheel in the same pit and we had sixteen loads of ammunition. Was 3 a.m before we turned in.

21st August

August 21

Zeppelin raid on Yorkshire

Good dugout in bank in front of guns. S.O.S 2.30 a.m, fired till 8 a.m - hot work - we were all about beat. The crack of one gun was enough, but two together – We were all deaf. We turned in after breakfast for a few hours sleep. The valley shelled heavy. Walk to old position with Jack Wringe. From there to <u>Templeau</u> saw Jock Cannon who at the time was on a course of aeroplane spotting with the anti aircraft battery. He was very keen on this spotting business. This battery wished to get him transferred to their battery, he wouldn't hear of it. Called at 60 pounder battery as Hesbecourt. They felt pleased with themselves having silenced eight German batteries that day. We fired after tea. German plane only a few hundred feet up flew over us while firing. We wondered what the verdict would be when it returned with reports and maybe photographs. We were pleased when we heard that it had met its fate lower down the valley.

22nd August

Wire cutting from an early hour until 2 p.m. This prearranged shoot also made the enemy lively. Sure they knew something was coming when they saw their wire going up. We received report that shooting was good and that very little wire was left. We in our turn were searched for, but that day none dropped unpleasantly near. At dusk, Wright and I made a trip up to Hargicourt and Villaret. These places were between the front line and second line trench. We had heard that there was plenty of fruit to be had and there was. We returned with a sandbag each full of plums etc. Whether worth the uncalled for risk, I do not know. At one part of

August 22
Air raid on Dover, Ramsgate and Margate

A 4.5 "How" IN ACTION

the road, was a big notice which said "Mind
your head, you are under German Observation."
We crawled along this dangerous part – could
hear the whistle of machine gun bullets over the
bank. We groped about in the garden as I
mentioned previously, fruit that year was
plentiful and it could be gathered in the dark
. At intervals a "Very" light would go up, making
the garden as light as day. The lights became
more frequent – a trench mortar bomb burst in
the garden fifty yards away. Wright was up in
a tree, nearly fell down saying "I'm sure I heard
Fritz say add fifty". We decided to go and it's
a good thing that we did – we returned to the
battery at 11 p.m. Ginger Wright was a queer
fellow. In England nothing could be done with
him, always in cells. But what a change. In
France he was one of the hardest working fellows

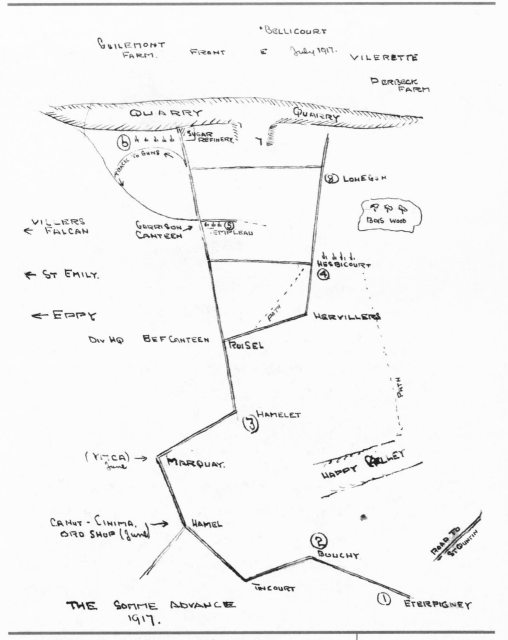

THE SOMME ADVANCE
1917.

in the battery. Acted as ambulance man. If
shells were falling like rain, he would be out in it.
He was awarded the Military Medal at Ypres,
and later was wounded. S.O.S at midnight.

HIGH EXPLOSIVE BURSTS.

23rd August

Wire cutting. Walked over to D Battery to see our old Brigade Sergeant Major Gregory. A and C Batteries shelled heavy. Also 197 Royal Horse Artillery Battery.

24th August

Wire cutting all day. Went down to quarry in afternoon. Drawing water from well. Water point shelled. Had to take cover. Many dead lying outside cemetery awaiting burial. A long line, all stitched up in their blankets. Also lines of ready dug graves- Not a cheerful sight. Right to the end the Army had their last draw in — The price of blanket and groundsheet was deducted from the money due to the soldier — and many a time this blanket was never used, but the price you may be sure was deducted from money due.

In afternoon had to go to Templeau to
Lincolnshire Infantry headquarters. Germans
made attack at night. <u>Gillemont Farm</u> lost.
This kept us busy. Had misfortune to get hot oil
in my eye. Eye very painful. Had to go to
dressing station.

25th August

Preparing for big barrage. Loads of ammunition
came up. The objective was Cologne farm, a
German stronghold.

26th August

Zero hour was a 4 a.m.. Since midnight we were
firing a "counter preparation". This being to
keep the enemy occupied. Was a damp misty
morning. Our valley was shelled heavy. We fired
until 10 a.m. The infantry gained their
objective but with heavy losses. Hundreds of
wounded passed by our guns. 300 Prisoners taken.
Our valley shelled heavy with 5.9 shells. The rain
made things more uncomfortable.

27th August

S.O.S all day. Many a counter attack was
launched against the Lincolnshire's line. But
Cologne farm was still ours. At night, went with
Wright to take signallers rations up to the second
line trench. An "infantry runner" led us up. All
quiet going up. signallers HQ (Headquarters) in

trench that Germans had held the previous day.
Enemy started "bumping" trench. The signallers
took us down in the dugout. A deep sap. Fitted
with beds and electric light. Sure the Germans
believed in comfort. This sap was sixty feet deep
with three tunnels and those branching off
forming little beds. The trench was badly blown
about. The reserve platoons were glad of this cover.
All were standing to. The "straff" above died
down a bit so we made our way back.

28th August

An easy day. Walked to main position at night.

29th August

An all day bombardment on Ruby Wood (on our
right front). "C" Battery shelled heavily for three
hours. Several wounded including Gunner York
(from my old battery)

30th August

Left for wagon line. We knew that the Division
was moving, but where to we really did not know,
but we could give a good guess.

1st September

Cleaning up. Cinema at Hamel at night

2nd September

Battery Parade Inspection by the C.O (Major O'Connell). The Major was an old soldier. Had seen a deal of service in France before joining us. A good man. Those old soldiers although a trifle fussy and strict on discipline were the best men when in actual warfare. They "knew the game" and took no uncalled for risks. Under them one had a feeling of safety and they always looked after the men better with regard to rations and comfort. While in France, I served under several different Majors. I well noticed the difference. Well O'Connell made a speech. Plenty of praise etc for past work. Of course there had to be that. These are extracts:

"You are now going to the Ypres Salient, you are about to take part in the greatest battle in the war and it will be the final battle. The enemy will be pushed over the Pilkem and Pa(sschendaele) Ridges and then we walk through (optimism!). Gas and continuous shelling you will experience. By your side will be England's most famous Regiments. You will cover the "Guards". The latter alone is an experience to be proud of. Gunners will be relieved every six days." (that was at the time something to look forward to).

September 1

Germany takes the northernmost end of the Russian front in the Riga offensive

The suggestion was well enough, but alas it was not put into practice. It was impossible. Nothing to be enthusiastic about in his speech. What did it matter who we covered, whether "the Guards" or any other line regiment. They all did their best and we did. The peacetime soldier was no better than a man of two years service when it came to actual warfare. Apart from the Major's speech, we knew full well what was in store for us. Sure the terrors of the "salient" were well known to all. But what did it matter, we would not be the only battery there. Poor old O'Connell did not last very long after passing through Menin Gate.

3rd September

Packing up. When preparing for a move this was a big task. A sack of corn and three trusses of hay had to be roped on to each wagon. Boxes of horse shoes, picquet lines – stakes etc, and everything had to be tidy.

WAGGON READY FOR ROAD.

Far different to the way the French .75 Battery used to turn out when on the move. To see them one would think it a circus. Have even seen the gunners sitting on the limbers with umbrellas up during a rain storm.

4th September

Finished packing. Moved off at 4 a.m, on to Peronne, We loaded up. Not a thankful job. Managed to get over to the Y.M.C.A. Took in a supply of cigarettes etc. At 4 p.m. the train moved off. On and on we went. Did not notice the route except that we passed through Amiens, a town where we had spent some happy hours. We sat there with our legs hanging over the side, interested in the countryside. The train travelled very slowly, stopping every now and then. I remember on one occasion, we stopped near a well loaded orchard. Rather silly I should imagine to cultivate fruit so near the railway. Darkness came on. We closed the door and settled down for the night.

THE TROOP
TRAIN.

5th September

Sound asleep we were when awoken by several loud crashes. Rather a rude awakening. We all aroused ourselves. We opened the sliding door of the truck. Was just getting light. We heard the drone of enemy machines overhead. The "anti aircraft" opened fire. A few more bombs dropped and then they went. The train was by a railway siding. How long we had been there I do not know. We settled down to sleep again until 6 a.m.. Unloaded. We inquired the name of the village, it was Proven a village on the Belgian frontier. Moved off at 10 a.m. Arrived at Wateau, a fair sized village. Quite different surroundings to what we had been used to. Very flat country. Long straight roads. Cobbles in the centre of roads. Hop vines. How strange seemed the Flemish wordings outside the shops and estaminets. The word "BIER-HAUS" seemed to cheer the lads up. Parked guns in field. Put up lines. I wandered round trying to find sleeping accommodation but failed to do so. This task was always left to me. A limber gunner had always plenty of time. No horses and no parades. So the detachment always left such affairs to their limber gunners. But at Wateau I was unlucky. Still there were plenty of stars at night. We found a nice little farm house at the end of the park. We hadn't a great deal

FLANDERS.

of money, but managed to collect enough for an
egg and chip supper, a favourite repast with the
troops — and very nice too. We slept under the
gun. The thunder of gunfire didn't worry us.
That would wait. A good night we had.

6th September

An easy day. Cleaned up. A nice day. Funds
were out so could not go out. We sat discussing our
whereabouts. How far we were from the line etc.
In the distance we could hear the never ending
gunfire, and way up in front was a long line of
observation balloons. In the afternoon I received a
surprise visit from Walter Brown (Barley, an old
chum of mine was in the 11th Division Royal
Engineers. He also was short of funds. I managed
to borrow 10 francs from Lieutenant Allways and
we had a good evening out. Of course, the boys

came too. Jock had some rum (he always had a reserve supply). We sampled a few wines, then it came time to depart. Brown was going out for rest. We were just going into it. On arriving back to Battery, we found Jack Wringe in rather a lively state. We were too. Was the first time had seen J.W so merry. But he was serious about it. " Where are my scouts" he was saying. (afterwards he was often reminded about his scouts). He had set his mind to "pinch" some sacks of oats off

"A" Battery's wagons. Why, I do not know. Jock, Inman and I complied with his wishes! We struggled with these sacks of corn. Why we were not heard I do not know, I guess it was a struggle considering we had had a night out. We settled down to sleep. Commenced to rain. In the darkness, we moved our place of abode to the doorway of a nearby cottage, but not for long. At the unearthly hour of 2 a.m we were called up.

7th September

A gale blowing. Pouring with rain. Moved off at 4 a.m. We felt quite cheerful I don't think. Daybreak was late, being such a miserable morning. The numerous dumps by the Roadside informed us that we were getting nearer. Yes, that and the rattle of gunfire. Tin houses. Yes really Tin — made from old biscuit tins. The abode of people who had been driven from their

homes further up. On we went. Passed through
the little town so well known to the men of the
"salient", Poperinge commonly known as "POP".
And at last arrived at the "field." I intended to
write. Better to describe it as a swamp. Nine
inches of slime, this was to serve as the wagon
line. Where it was, I do not know. Never troubled
to enquire. Where we slept that night I do not
remember. No note of it in my diary, no sleep at
all perhaps. An awful "straff" was going on in
front and at night the sky was a blaze of light.
Not very inviting I can assure you. The right
section went up. Four horses and one man killed
going up.

8th September

Pay day. Found coffee house and walked along
main road to Y.M.C.A. This building had been
provided by Trinity College Cambridge. Around
the walls hung familiar views of the old varsity
town. Quite homelike. We got into conversation
with a man who had seen a good deal of the
salient. I well remember his words: "you are
artillery men, aren't you? I pity you – the
average life of an artillery man up here is two
weeks". Very cheerful, I admit. Still he was right.
We often recalled his words. We returned to the
wagon line. During dinner, several long-range
shells dropped at far end of horse lines. No

damage. Lorry came up with packs for the horses and in the late afternoon, we (the left and central section) moved up.

Now the 8th of September we went into the salient with full strength. Feeling fit and health good, and we returned on October 4th minus half the original battery and those that did remain were absolutely worn out. My diary during this time was not kept up to its standard. I hardly thought that I should ever survive to read it. A waste of time to carry on with it, so will relate from memory a few incidents which happened. Will carry on with the diary part later.

As to the salient — a small semi-circular district whose diameter was eight miles of canal that ran through Ypres (north and south) and whose circumference was the line of trenches from Pilkem, out to Hooge, three miles east of Ypres, and down to St Eloi. Three main roads branched out into the salient. Roads of death. Ghastly sights were to be seen at every turn. These roads Menin Way, Zillebeke and St. Jean. From these main roads ran by-roads. Perhaps they did not exist in pre-war days. The points at which these by-roads joined the main roads, were well registered by the enemy. Day and night they were shelled. Renowned corners were "Salvation Corner", Hellfire corner", "Oxford Circus" and "Iron Cross Corner". Into this crowded area divisions and army corps were herded to take part in the third battle of Ypres. So thick, that very few enemy shells and bombs were wasted. During the day the roads were not used much, all being under observation. But from dusk until day-break it was a continual procession. To walk along these roads at dawn — what ghastly sights. Men and horses which had been killed, and run over thousands of times by the heavy traffic. And when the weather became worse, tracks were made with railway sleepers. Many a time I have seen these sleepers floating. If a wagon ran off the track, there was no getting it back. Had to be pushed off into the mud. One breakdown would perhaps cause to halt three miles of traffic and to halt on these ever shelled tracks was not healthy. Dead horses and men were no good to anyone. They were dumped by the side of the track and left. At one point, I well remember a pile of dead men and horses and it is a fact a fortnight later, when we passed, they were still there. We became accustomed to this frightfulness. Still, the dead were dead. And perhaps others would have also lost their lives burying the men I have mentioned. The mud. One could get killed by shell and bullet on other fronts, but in Ypres one could also have drowned. I have seen men up to their shoulders in shell holes, have helped to pull them out with ropes. Of course (some) have sunk so deep they had to be shot. There were no trenches, shell holes being the only cover. The enemy used every method possible to hold the line and this he managed to do. Gas, sometimes six or seven hours at a stretch. Fire shells that were used to fire ammunition dumps, aerial torpedos. shells that had a burst like that of a munitions factory going up. Gothas bombed the trenches and guns both by day and night. He was paid back in the same coin. As to our front: guns (they) were about eight yards apart. Long lines of them as far as (one) could see and from front to rear about two hundred yards between. Right back beyond Ypres, ammunition wagons could not be used. Shells were brought up on pack horses. (8 shells per horse).

THE REMAINS OF THE FAMOUS CLOTH HALL YPRES

It was work, work, work. Yes, work to live. They had to be kept back. Sleep we learned to do without – no time to even think about it. One describes it as an artillery battle. It was. Guns against guns. The infantry even said that it was safer in the their so-called trenches. We went into action full strength. Including officers and signallers the gun line strength was about forty-six men. Five men on each gun. Day by day, the strength grew less, our average losses were six each day. We would dwindle down to two men per gun. Was killing work when so short handed; What hopes of our relief every six days? Reinforcements would come up and again the strength would diminish. One gunner, I never did know his name, was killed on our gun had only come up two hours previous. And there were like instances on other guns. It was "one killed and two wounded on B gun". "Who were they?" "Er soand so, and

two new men". At the end, there were about
eight of us old gunners left and had lost in all,
about fifty.

12" HOW ON RAILWAY MOUNTING
AT YPRES.

I think that all dreaded the night. The noise was
greater and the distance was deceiving. A shell a
hundred yards away would sound as though
bursting between the guns. If one was unoccupied
and unable to sleep (by that I mean that the
battery was "standing to") the minutes seemed
like hours. Terrible sights one saw with the
wounded. One instance I remember was a
bombardier, both legs were shattered asking an
officer to shoot him. Was a hard job to get the
wounded away. These dead were taken to rear in
the cook's cart. This cart seldom went back
empty. Food was plentiful, and (we) were well
doctored up with rum. As to the weather: the
first two weeks we had perfect autumn weather.
Really hot, day and night we only wore shorts
and shirts. On a gun one could always keep
warm. Was seldom that we had a wash and as to

shaving, that too was out of the question. If only photos could have been taken of us. I mentioned before that our greatest trouble was the "chats". Lack of time to spend on the "hunts". These insects thrived. Jock used to say that they were attacking "in mass formation".

And then came the rain, day and night it rained. Seemed as though it would never cease. The "salient" became a sea of mud forever being churned up by bursting shells. The guns sank in. Ammunition coated with slime and ourselves too. Round the guns we laid thicket fences; these sank. Many a time it was up to our knees. Ypres at its "best."

THE OLD MILL NEAR VLAMERTINGHE

8th September continued

Left wagon line at 5 p.m. On we went along the old cobble road. As far as one could see was a line of moving. We passed the old Mill Tower (used as a dressing station). Quite a landmark in that quarter. A few long-range shells burst to our right, being two hundred yards beyond their

mark. Passed through <u>Vlamertinge</u>, a shattered
village. The tall ghostly looking mass of brickwork
standing at the corner, we recognised as the
church. A big twelve inch gun mounted on rails
to the left of road, and in front we had our first
glimpse of the fated city Ypres. On entering we
received instructions from the traffic police to
keep a space of fifty yards between each team
and we entered <u>Ypres</u>. Am afraid that I cannot
describe the town. I saw but little of it, but quite
enough. I remember passing the remains of the
Cathedral and the Cloth Hall. Nothing else. <u>Ypres</u>
was being shelled. The traffic in front went off
at a trot, and we followed. With the crash of
shells and fumes it was rather unhealthy.
Impossible to term it a sightseeing expedition. We
turned right at "<u>Hell Fire Corner</u>". It well
merited its name. At this corner, very few
German shells were wasted. Our gun and wagons
got by well, but "F" sub happened unlucky. Three
horses were killed. We Gunners went back to help
them. Not a thankful occupation at such a spot.
We cut out the dead horses. (All harness was
fitted with what was known as "quick release" so
that the horses could be freed at once). We
cleared the dead horses off the road at the same
time keeping under cover as best we could. It was
then dark of course. Along Menin Road, as far
as "<u>Eight Inch Corner</u>," turned right up the

<u>Cambridge Road</u>, and left along the track to
"Potsdam Farm". And what a reception. Had
just unhooked guns, when the gas signals were
rung. Not a long spell. Our first experience.

ANOTHER LOUD SPEAKER!

a 9·2 GUN ON ROAD MOUNTING

Happened at an awkward time. Our guns we
had to pull in position. Ammunition we had to
unload. Gas or not, horses had to be got away.
Skipper Clark was gassed. After the gas the
enemy attacked. I was returning from the
Cambridge Road at the time, having guided the
teams to main road, picking the way between
the shell-holes. S.O.S lights went up and the music
commenced. I happened to be passing by a gun of
"C" battery when it opened fire. I did not know
it was there. Must have been level with my eye.
Biggest shock I have ever had. In scrambling
away, I slipped into a water filled shell-hole.
Luckily it was not so deep as some. Was thankful

when I arrived back to the position. All the time, the barrage continued. One cannot describe it, was as light as day with the flashes. The noise — was impossible to hear one speak. The heavy boom of the heavies, the sharp cracks of the eighteen pounders and the air seemed full of screeching howling monsters. So much was the air disturbed we could even feel it. Guns — there must have been thousands of them. We did not fire. We, after the "straff" had died down covered up. Found a convenient shell hole, spread our blankets out and settled down for the night. Beddington came around. He was then Officer in charge of the left section. Rather a babyish voice he had, said: "the Boche will see you, you must get up at daybreak." The answer he received, I will not relate. We slept, and were not disturbed. Shells had dropped near, but we did not hear them. We knew that they had dropped fairly close as we found quite a collection of shrapnel on top of our "bed".

9th September

It was eight a.m. before we roused ourselves. Did not take Beddington's advice. A beautiful day — hot. German planes busy. No need to worry about them on the Ypres front. Batteries were seldom marked individually. Put up camouflage, filled sandbags and made a rough wall around the gun. This wall no doubt saved us on many occasions. Well, (in the) afternoon we had to keep low. The ridge, thirty yards in front was shelled continu(ously). Plenty of work there was to be done, but "safety first" was the motto. Well into the night we carried on with dump making. About twelve to each gun and a good space between each. As to position: Two hundred yards east of <u>Cambridge Road</u>. The Road to <u>Potsdam Farm</u> passed through the battery at right angles (passing between C and D guns). Behind us was a trench – hardly a trench – better describes as a mound such as one sees bordering a dyke.

This idea:

The trench part was always twelve inches deep with water. While at this position, the weather was good. In the trench, we made a false bottom with duckboards and dug pits to drain the water. Even in the dry weather water was only eighteen inches under (the) surface. Cookhouse was at "A". A hole in which to sleep 3 men, we dug at "B". small dumps we also dug in east bank. The crest in front was under direct observation of the enemy. From there, could be seen the German line; a line of deep "saps" thirty feet deep had been constructed on east side of Cambridge Road. Pumps worked by small oil engines we kept busy day and night. To our left was Eight Inch Corner (conjunction of the Cambridge, Oxford and Menin Roads) – a lively corner too.

10th September

We fired on and off all day. Again, the ridge was shelled. Nearly hit when out for lamp. At 9 p.m, we were shelled heavy by a 5.9 battery. At the time, several wagons of ammunition were passing along the track between guns. (Wagons belonging to the 4.5 howitzer battery in front). Eight horses killed and two men. Several wounded. Several of us ran down to the scene of the accident. Released the live horses. They ran off. With the aid of electric lamp we found the wounded. Dragged them to shelter. Shells were dropping thickly. We crawled along trench.

When opposite cookhouse (cookhouse stood on side of huge shell-hole). Shell burst in this hole. We were absolutely covered with slime thrown out by the burst. We sought shelter. Crawled, Douglas and I in a little shelter in side of the bank. A boarded front. This place we had not previously investigated. Contained a number of boxes. In this place we crawled, the shelling still continued. Another shell blew in part of the trench and boarded side of our shelter splintered . Must have missed us by inches.

YPRES.

We moved again. Crawled further along trench. Ordered to clear away from the battery, but was a deal softer to remain. Lieutenant Marshal came by. Said that we had to clear. Asked if we hadn't heard the order. Off he went. Next we heard that he had been badly wounded. (died later). Dump in our pit set alight . Douglas and I managed to put it out with wet scrim (a painted sacking material). Hand and arm were cut by brass splinters from the case. Sergeant Frith and two "B sub" gunners wounded. B and C guns hit at midnight. All was quiet again. We settled down for a few hours of sleep.

11th september

Up at daybreak. Until breakfast time were busy clearing the remains of the horses killed the night before. What a job it was. Believe me not a

A SHELL CARRIER

healthy job to tackle before breakfast. No need to dig holes. Enough shell holes in the vicinity. Each large enough to hold another half dozen such carcasses. A messy job. I remember finding the hand of one of the unlucky drivers cut off, as if by a knife. This too went in with the horses. The day went on. Heavily we were shelled. Even deprived of our dinner. What rough times the cooks had. No picnic preparing meals under such conditions. Water scarce. The amount of smoke restricted, and it was he who got scowls if meals were not up to the mark or "a la Ritz" as we were used to say. Still, they served us real well. If nothing else in the Salient, one could eat. A rough afternoon. We had Gunner Chantry and Major O'Connell killed. Lofthouse and another gunner wounded. "C" gun was hit badly and at night we were entertained by a six hour gas attack - mustard gas. Amongst the bursts one could detect some that fell with a thud and followed this a hissing sound. A hitching (itching) feeling in the nose and the Salient would sound like a cup tie match. The sounding of gongs (these being empty

shell cases) and rattles, quite a din. On would go
the helmets. Shells would fall thick and heavy.
Yes, thick and heavy they would fall. At
intervals, we would "test the air", lift up the
mask and sniff – and believe me at times it
WAS thick. Take a good sniff at a tin of
"Colemans" and you have got it. When not in
action, it was not so bad. Was possible to sleep in
the masks. Rather a sensation to wake up and
wonder what the D.... had happened to your face.
In action, these masks were a nuisance. Couldn't
see well. Eyes from time to time had to be
uncovered. Had to suffer for it the next day. So
much for gas.

Was a quieter night. Went in front of ridge at
night spotting flashes and timing the distance
from the bursts. Very interesting. Lieutenant
Beddington was making reports. I now forget how
they were calculated.

12th September

A quieter day. Batteries to left and right were
shelled heavily. We were still sleeping (when lucky
in the shell hole in the gunpit.) The shrapnel
that lay on our blankets in the morning, did not
exactly please us., so we decided to make a bit of
shelter. In the trench, we dug down twelve inches.
Over the grave-like hole we laid a sheet of
elephant iron, and walled it in with a double

wall of sandbags. Only enough room for two. This we decided should be the shelter for those who had to spend the night in the pit. (Until now we had all been doing so). In the afternoon, we started on a small dugout in the side of the trench. Until late we worked, and at last we were respectably housed. Of course, there was a deal more shelter in the trench, so we decided to do "pit duty" in turns. Doug and I did first. Matter of fact we all did it. Fired all night. Ammunition came up. At 4 a.m. (it) was still dark. Shells were falling in the vicinity. This we more fully realised when a horse was killed and the driver wounded when unloading at our gun. This burst in question, none of us noticed.

POSITION AT CAMBRIDGE ROAD

13th September

Wormleighton (Corporal) took charge of our gun. Jack Wringe took over Sergeant Major of gun line. A lively day. Two wounded in right section. Jock and Crowdens turn to sleep in pit. Douglas,

Wormleighton and I in trench "bivi" All was quiet. This being so, we turned in early and we slept. shells might fall, but what did it matter if one was asleep. And a good night we had. But it appears that our pals in the pit did not fare so well. At some unearthly hour, they were awakened by Jock saying that the camouflage had been blown down. The answer that he received I will not write. (Soldiers had a language of their own) But at daybreak, we did get up. "Now what is the matter"? we enquired and were conducted to the pit. What a shock, but I guess that the shock of Jock had been greater. A 4.2 shell had burst in the pit. Gun half turned over had missed their shelter by inches. In fact it stood on the edge of the shell hole. The sandbags at side of wall were torn to ribbons. Camouflage was destroyed and two dumps were missing. No wonder they were worried.

14th September

Jock vowed that he would never sleep in the pit again and he never did. He said "He's sure to have got the line". Anyway he was lucky to have escaped. We set to repairing the damage. New camouflage we created, and by 10 a.m all was straight. We had just made some tea and the five of us were standing outside "the cookhouse." A huge shell burst over on the Cambridge Road.

We were watching the curling mass of smoke,
when we heard a fragment coming. Heard it,
but felt as though we could not move. Crowden
fell down, hit. Not a bad wound - a nice
"Blighty one". A rough afternoon we had. "C"
gun blown up. A pile of scrap metal remained
and "A" gun damaged.

15th September

Ammunition unloading from packs. 2.30 a.m to
5 a.m. One horse hit. The horse fell on bomb.
Shelled heavy in the afternoon. Gunner Robinson
killed and 3 signallers wounded.

16th September

A surprise for us. An order came through that
B295 had to rest for two days. No work was to be
done, and even if there was an S.O.S we had not
to fire, but guns and men had to remain in
line. A certain few were to be taken for a day to
POP. We cut cards for it. I was one of the lucky
ones. Two General Service Wagons came up. And
we set off. Was just after daybreak. Back
through Ypres. Things were fairly quiet. Was
light. When at Ypres could take a closer look at
the surroundings.. Nothing much of interest
except for the ramparts at the Menin gate, and
the canal. A grand day it was. Called at wagon
line. Rum issue- POP at last. A town of the real

Flemish type. Plenty of civilians. Shops all
boarded up. Rather a big risk for them to
remain there, but the(y) must have been doing
a "roaring trade". Estaminets with their
mechanical organs. We had a good time. First
good wash we had since arriving in the Salient.
We dined well, and spent the greater part of the
day in the estaminets. Visited the canteen to
buy stores for those who remained, including some
wine and beer. During the afternoon, some long-
range shells fell in the town. Never have I seen
streets empty themselves so quick. A dive for the
cellars.

We met the wagons at 6 p.m. and started on our
journey back. Needless to say we "had a few".
Called at the wagon line. A rum issue. This
about finished us. We lay in the bottom of the
wagon and remembered no more until we arrived
at the position. "Hell Fire Corner" did not worry
us that night. The joke was that afterwards a
traffic police looked in the wagon and that he
informed the drivers that they were travelling in
the wrong direction. That the cemetery was on
the west of Ypres. Hardly so bad.

17th September

Up early. Four of us walked over to the crest in
front. With a pair of field glasses we surveyed the
line. In the distance behind the German Line

could be seen green fields, undamaged houses,
spires of churches, etc. After a while, the ridge
was heavily shelled. We found shelter in a
somewhat dilapidated tank. Not much left of it.
Holes had been cut through the thick armour
plate as though it had been matchwood. Shells
dropped round. Still we were safe except for a
direct hit. We returned for dinner. Had just
finished dinner, when a flight of Gothas came
over escorted by fighting machines flying low
below the elevation of the anti aircraft batteries.
I assure you that we kept low. I did not notice
where the bombs dropped. Anyway, too close to be
pleasant. With bomb bursts, one was forced to
keep low. The bombs were fitted with
instantaneous detonators which burst at first
contact. The contents spread horizontally. Hardly
a ground mark was visible. When the excitement
was over, made up my mind to visit Freestone in
B296 Battery about three quarters of a mile
away. Could see the position quite well from the
Potsdam track. What a time it took to get
there. Cambridge Road was being "bumped"
heavy. Many a time I had to take shelter. At
the same time, B296 were getting it heavy. I sat
down in a shell hole and waited for it to quieten
down. Freestone I met. Was strange, he hardly
recognised me. No wonder perhaps, judging from
my appearance, clothes etc, clad only in shorts

and what remained of a shirt. In that
particular straff, they lost three men. Freestone I
found fishing his officer's kit out from a dugout
that had stopped a 4.2 (He was the officer's
servant). I helped him to clear up. Shaving soap
etc. Came very acceptable.

After a talk, I wandered back. Road was then
quiet, but not for long. Battery had a severe
'straffing' "D" Gun was blown to pieces. Four men
lost. The salient was getting rougher. An awful
night. Impossible to sleep. Gas for six hours.

18th and 19th September

The commencement of the Menin Road battle or
the Third Battle of Ypres. Started firing at 3
a.m, and continued for twenty four hours
without stop. Were covering the Australians,
South Africans and 9 Division. They captured
their objective but with heavy losses. S.O.S for
hours. As fast as shells could be carried to guns,
they were fired. At intervals, we had to rest.

Cooling the guns down with pails of water. So hot it used to be that when pulling through, the mop was scorched. The burns that we got on our hands and arms were many and the gas burns too. The very ground was tainted with gas. The soil on which a gas shell had burst would fetch up blisters. On a damp night, the gas would hang on our clothes and where the clothes touched the skin was burned off especially at the wrists.

20th September

Early morning, a German plane "machine gunned" our teams when leaving position. A quieter day, but no rest for us. We were kept busy filling up our stores with ammunition. We had sent some stuff over during the bombardment. I wonder what damage we really did. We averaged about six thousand shells per gun per day. Tons of stuff were thrown over to be divided amongst them. Up all night. Our fourth without sleep.

21st September

Rain, a hot muggy day. During the night, the horses that we buried so nicely on the 10th were blown out. I do not think that I have ever seen a more horrible mess. And the sickly smell that accompanied it. We scraped them back again. The Germans commenced to use a fifteen inch gun. Bursts to rear more like the explosion of a

munitions factory going up. We were thankful
that he kept a good range. In the evening, went
down to Cambridge Road for some sandbags. Met
Gunner Green (afterwards killed) with three
more carrying a stretcher. Green informed me
that it was a chum of mine on the stretcher,
dead. I lifted the cover. Gunner Hughes of A295,
one of the old Herts. Boys.

23rd September

Orders came for us to change over with a battery
on our left perhaps two miles away. Why the
changeover had to be, I do not know. We changed
over in sections, Right section first. Guns were not
moved. We were to take over theirs and they were
to take over ours. We, the left section, were the
last to leave and in broad daylight. The relieving
battery brought up pack horses. The enemy
balloons were up all the time. And the fun began.
I was at the gun at the time – talking to
Bombardier Fowler who stood in the hollow
between the bank and pit.

TRENCH
MORTAR.

shells were falling thick between battery and road. These did not matter much, but all at once there was a roar. I made a dive. Luckily managed to get half in the little shelter, a sort of earthquake sensation. The sandbag sides fell in. The Battery had in the meantime, cleared away from guns, and I crawled away from shell hole to shell hole. A poor chance of surviving in such a straff. When clear, I took note of what had happened. My puttees were splashed with blood. Whether I was wounded, I did not know. Had received several nasty knocks and could feel them. I took off puttees. Everything all right. And then I remembered Bombardier Fowler who I'd been talking to. I made my way to "Eight Inch Corner". Met Douglas and Jock, and together, we went back. Was strange they had already heard that I had been killed. Bashford of "B" sub was last to leave position. He saw me just before the gun was hit, saw that someone had been killed and concluded that it was me. This he reported to the others at the new position. Quite a welcome I received when I joined them. The excitement was now finished. We viewed the destruction. The 4.2 had burst in exactly the same place as before when Jock was sleeping in the pit. The camouflage had been burned. Two dumps blown up, shells complete with case had been blown a distance of one hundred yards. My personal kit

and tools of the gun had disappeared. Gun was
but little damaged. I realised what an escape I
had had.

SAND BAG CORNER.
YPRES.

A gun was hit too. Cookhouse had stopped a shell.
As to Bombardier Fowler, the largest piece I
remember seeing of him was a piece of leg from
knee to ankle. It took nearly two hours to cover up
the pieces. The tiny pieces of flesh covered the
ground for yards around. "A" Battery on the
road had many killed and wounded during the
same straff. The packs and men that had
caused all the trouble – I really do not know how
they fared. I saw several dead horses behind the
right section guns. At 3 p.m we walked over to
our new position. Down Oxford Road, Admiral
Road, Sandbag Corner, to turning off St Julian
Road. District was known as Weilty. A gun stood
just to left of road, and battery extended to left.
Guns ten yards apart. And depth front to rear
was about forty yards.

23rd – 24th September

Sandbag walls had been built round guns.
Improvement could be made. Had just arrived,
when we had S.O.S some straff – the noise was
greater than on Cambridge Road. In the evening,
we saw the biggest air fight yet seen. About
thirty planes took part and seven planes were
destroyed. We slept an hour or so under the gun.
At 3 A.M. we were heavily shelled. "B" sub
dugout blown in. Three killed including Morris.
Several wounded. Was until daybreak digging
them out. The wounded we carried to aid post by
Sandbag Corner. Fired nearly all day. The
salient was getting worse day by day. All day we
could hardly move for shelling. Aid post on our
left was blown up. Started making a rough "bivi"
in rear of gun.

AN AID POST
IN A GERMAN PILL BOX.

Jenkins was "shell shocked". Nearly went mad. 5.9
shells were falling on the position at the time.
Took six of us to hold him down. Finally, we
strapped him to a stretcher. In the evening, Doug
and I walked up to dump on St Julian Road for

sandbags. Our teams passed us with ammunition. They had just arrived when the "music" started again. I hardly remember such another "straff". Heavy stuff and a few fire shells included. We hurried back to get the horses out of it. The shells we threw out on the side of the road. Two horses were killed, and four drivers wounded. I had a splinter hit my knee. Nothing more than a bruise. A large dump of "very" lights was fired on our left. Jock went down sick. Sleep was impossible that night.

25th September

A rough day. Germans busied themselves with curtain barrages, starting at Ypres and creeping slowly up. Three times did we have to leave battery. Were lucky to have a trench forty yards in front of guns. This was very useful. Had to shelter there at night. I had the misfortune to fall from bank. Stepped onto a trench mortar bomb. My arm still bears witness to that fall — felt very cheerful with a stiff arm and leg. At night we were entertained with a seven hour gas attack.

26th September

At dinner time, while firing, we were bombed by Gothas. Bombardier Walton wounded. A lovely night. Bright moonlight. The bombers were busy.

September 26

Polygon Wood fell to the Australians and Tower Hamlets was captured by the British

Very low they flew. Jack Wringe and we standing
near the road thought it advisable to lie down.
Our shadows we thought were rather conspicuous.
Lucky for us we did. A bomb burst ten yards
away, killing the cooks cart horse.

27th September — 6th October

Things became worse. Rain came on — mud —
what a mess. My diary suffered. No time for
diaries. Night and day work . Our casualties
were many. The Guards made their big attack
preceded with a twenty-four hour bombardment.
They had S.O.S lasted for hours. Heavy losses.
Trenches were lost and regained every night. We
would drop the range to as much as five hundred
yards then creep up again — Tanks crawled
through the mud to help but the Germans could
not be moved. We were all feeling the effects.

a 18 inch
How

Inman had joined "C" sub. We were at the time
very short handed. The barrage had to be kept

up. Gunfire during the S.O.S.s. Firing as quick as we could put them in the breech and then we were asked if we could get them off quicker. "Quicken up" was often the order. I caught 'flu' and quickly became worse and at last collapsed. Couldn't be moved down, so in "Bivi" behind the gun I remained. No strength to move. This billet was a sheet of elephant iron with sandbag walls covered with a sheet of wet essen (hessian) to keep out the gas. I remember during the numerous times the battery was shelled, covering my head up with blankets. The heavy thuds get on ones nerves. Was impossible to keep a candle alight. Doug would come in, warn me that the battery had to clear out "are you coming"? For my part, he could have dropped a shell on the place. That was how I felt at the time. And Douglas too would not leave. "If you don't clear I don't" he would say. In the meantime, I got gassed. Was on the 4th October, I heard that my old chum was bad with gas. Billy Buck, I went to see him. He died on the position. Took my helmet off for a few moments and the usual results followed. Lost my voice, and my eyes gradually grew worse. On the 7th I was put on an 'off' horse. This horse ran away. Rather an adventurous ride. The horse knew his way back to the wagon line. Was more than I did. Slept night in the wet slimy wagon at <u>Ondank</u>. Bombed at night. Still I didn't

remember much. As to other Ypres incidents.
Inman received the Military medal for rescuing
three wounded men from "C" sub pit, which had
been hit by a gas shell. He was also badly gassed.
(He died from the effects later in 1920).

8th October

Sent down to the divisional hospital at <u>Lovie</u>.
Near POP. Near the Deputy Adjutant General
Headquarters. Could hardly speak, and couldn't
see to read. Quite comfortable beds. Warm. (La
Lovie Chateau was some 2 1/2 kilometres from
Poperinghe. It was headquarters for many B.E.F.
units, and George V stayed there in July 1917)

13th October

Felt much better. Voice still missing. Up the line
again. Position was then at <u>Langemarke</u>. Firing
at close range — The boys had it rough during
the while I had been away. What a mess, we're
up to our knees in a sea of mud. Guns were
nearly up to their axles. Shells could only be fired
at about two per minute, and every shell had to
be washed before putting into the breech. Sammy
Starling wounded. Was carrying a thicket fence.
Was hit. One could nearly term it as amusing to
see him roll back in the mud and the thicket on
top of him. If it had been night and he had
been alone, he would have certainly been drowned.

Poor old Sammy. Was an awful day. What with the rain, mud and shelling. The cookhouse was nearly half a mile to the rear in a sandbag trench. Two of us went to fetch the tea. This was prepared in a large tin (five gallons) constructed on the Thermus (Thermos) Flask principle – As we picked our way over the floating duck boards, my chum (forgot who he was) said: "I am hit". A shell certainly had dropped unpleasantly near. He was carrying the can on his shoulder at the time. We set the can down and made investigations. He wasn't hit himself, but the can had been punctured and hot tea was trickling down his back.

14th October

We received the glad tidings that we were to bid farewell to the Salient. Jock said "not so much of your rejoicing until you get on the safe side of Cloth Hall". In the afternoon, the 34th Division came up, took over our position. We did not stop to hear whether it pleased them or not. Very little could be seen of the guns. In another two or three days of such weather, they should have disappeared from view. "A" gun was out of action, having stopped a direct hit and we made our own way back, arriving at the wagon line at 8 p.m. Found a dry spot. Put up our trench sheet and were soon asleep.

As to other incidents: Daybreak at the gun line, as many as thirty horses would be found wandering about in the close vicinity, having escaped from their drivers during the night. Was no joke for them, leading a couple of horses through the mud. A shell would burst near, and off they would go. "C" battery on one occasion lost a gun. It was being taken up. Either the horses were killed or they couldn't move it out of the mud. They left it, intending to fetch it at daybreak. Major Ackermann of "A" Battery saw it. He was a gun short. He had it out. I can imagine the surprise when "C" Battery went to retrieve it and found it missing.

MUD!

The guns were pulled from the road at Iron Cross Corner by the Guards. Was hopeless for horses. Mules did good work in the Salient. For a wagon, it was always six horses or four mules; and if the wagon became stuck, many a time a team of mules had to be hooked in instead of the horses. Duck-boards were the only tracks to the trenches. Men were kept by day and night replacing the damaged ones. Was a job to get the wounded away. While on the St Julian Road, during a barrage, we had two wounded. We took them down to a PILL BOX where a party of Royal Army Medical Corps had headquarters.

STRETCHER BEARERS.!

This then about 6 a.m. At 3 p.m they were still there. Our men carried them further down. Many lay there all night and died. The infantry had a job to get out of it. I saw a man on the ridge. I went out to him. Had a bullet in his knee and said that he had crawled from the trenches. On one occasion, while groping my way over to the aiming post (night-time) I stumbled on a dead guardsman. Caught him with my toes. I fell with my knees on his body. A creepy sort of groan. Not a pleasant sensation. Another night we heard a call. A wounded man. We carried him to our billet, bandaged him, made him comfortable. Meant to take him to aid-post but gas came on. Lay down by his side, slept. Surprised to find him dead when trying to wake him in the morning. The life there was full of such incidents. Never a dull moment. Only a few I have related.

15th October

Rain – we were used to it. Rain or not, we were thankful that we were leaving the salient and how strange it seemed. So many old faces had gone – and there were new ones. These new men were as yet not allotted out to the various subsections. We moved off at 8 a.m. Was very difficult getting out of field owing to the mud and heavy loads. Back we went to <u>Eecke</u> having passed through POP. Guns parked in the fields opposite the Casino Estaminet. Found a good billet – in barn. – plenty of straw. After a few hours in the "casino" we retired and slept well – who wouldn't.

16th October

Moved off. Passed through <u>Hazelbrook</u>, (Hazebrook) a fair-sized town. Not much damaged. I forget the name of the place where we stayed.

17th October

Moved off at 8 a.m. A long march. Stayed the night at <u>Dommen</u> in loft above farm. Wire beds and very comfortable too. Spent evening in Y.M.C.A.

18th October

On we went through <u>Bethune</u>. Not damaged at all. A real holiday town for those on the Lens front. Passed the well-known landmark the Mill on the Hill near <u>Gouy Servins</u>. Arrived at wagon line at <u>Ablain St. Nazare</u> near <u>Souchy</u> (Souchez). These two places are well known. <u>Ablain</u> stood in a valley. On the north side, the valley side was at least 400 feet high. The advance party had procured tents for us – these we erected. Being tired after the long march, we retired to "bed" early, not worrying what tomorrow might bring. We knew that it would be action.

19th October

A lovely morning. The new gunners were allotted out. To our subsection came Ablett. I remember now how we eyed him up and down. Anyway, we made his acquaintance – wondered if he would be "one of us". We left the guns behind and walked up to <u>Leiven</u>. Relieving the Canadians.

Left kits at "Red Mill Siding" on light railway, and walked across to position. Viewed our new home. Asked the Canadians what the front was like. From their remarks we concluded that we were in for a holiday. The Canadians were bound for Ypres. Asked what it was like, could only wish them luck. Walked down to siding for our kits. Allway asked Jock to look after his kit – Jock said to us "I'm a fighting soldier, not a .... officer's servant, anyway he will be sorry that he left it with me". We helped to sort it out. One parcel Jock "lost". We "searched" for it everywhere. Anyway we were not sorry that Jock had been asked to look after the kit. Chocolates and biscuits. Many a laugh about Jock's duty as an officer's servant. Ablett our newcomer quite in earnest helped to search for the parcel and was surprised when it was produced in the evening. At an early hour we turned in.

19th – 22nd October

This turned out to be an easy front. A real holiday camp. Nothing exciting happened, nothing much of interest to record in the diary. Same routine, day after day. Dates of interest only I recorded. Here is a description of the position. 200 yards west of Leiven Church, on outskirts of town. On right front the ruins of an old chateau. Town not so very badly damaged (in comparison to other towns.) Had been a mining centre. Several mine heads or "Fosses" in the Town and district. Two mile in front was Lens, trenches being on the outskirts of Lens. The position was well spread out, four hundred yards between "A" and "E" guns. "F" gun was on track to Red Mill Siding two hundred yards away. The gun pits had been well made. "B" sub using an old German concrete pit. Our pit was in the cellar of the house. The walls above had been pulled over, forming a practically shell-proof roof. The cellar steps made a fine entrance to the pit.

This is the idea:

The roof was supported by elephant iron. On left of the gun was our billet. This too being a cellar. Above the cellar was a "lean to" building this was at first without a roof. We saw that this could be made into a comfortable living room. During the days that followed, we converted it to our liking. We "scrounged" round. Was easy here. Within ten minutes any required piece of furniture or cooking utensil could be found. We tiled the roof with cement and bricks. We made a huge fire place. What fires we used to have. Half a railway sleeper at a time. Day and night we always had a good fire. The room we equipped with table, chairs, cupboards, framed picture, stained glass window we won from the church, curtains, and even a white tablecloth. The cellar below was equipped with wire beds, not enough, but I later constructed new ones. A lovely war it was on the Lens Front. We made great improvements to the gun pit. As to firing, the average per gun was only sixty shells per week, and our gun fired the greatest percentage. We were termed as the "sniping" gun. Great fun our observing officers must have had during these sniping stunts. Often we were praised for good shooting. Notified on many occasions that we had scored direct hits. In middle of battery was a huge "sap". One entrance being in the cemetery on right of "A" and "B" subs. Slept in this "sap." One could walk through Leiven underground from cellar to cellar. The Germans had prepared all this at least three feet of concrete covered these cellars. In the town were several Y.M.C.A.s and canteens. One canteen was in an old hotel complete with bar and beer pumps, chairs and tables.

23rd October

60 pounder battery on left shelled heavy. A few shells fell near, with flying brick fragments. It seemed worse than it really was. Apart from this,

no other shell fell within half mile of position. The Canadians had left behind a good supply of oatmeal, rice and tea. This came in handy for our suppers. A bath house we constructed, scrounged several furnace pans with cement and bricks. We built some serviceable coppers. These were useful too for our washing days. Our living room was a huge success. Even the officers spent evenings with us. Very much they would have liked to have taken it over. Gramophone concerts and sing songs. All went well.

30th October

The gunners received rather depressing news. They were to go down to the wagon line to build stables. Jack Wringe put in a good word for me. I was detailed to remain behind with Ruddock and Blackburn. We were to look after the guns B and I. Ruddock was signaller. His job was to remain within hearing of the telephone. In front we had two reserve positions already constructed. These we had to visit every other day while the battery was away. This morning, Major Mausley (then our O.C.) took us with him to show us the reserve positions. From first position we went to the observation post observing position, a trench on a hill. The major told us to wait for him. We, curious as ever to know more of our surroundings. We sat on the parapet of the trench. In front of

October 24

Austria-Germany breakthrough at Caporetto on Italian front

October 30

Passchendaele Ridge was cleared of the enemy

us was Lens. The Major returned. He nearly exploded. "Don't you know that this is the O.P (news to us) Don't you know that you are three quarters of a mile from the German trenches and under direct observation?" We scrambled down quick enough. On we went, passing through well kept trenches (known as the Crocodile, Crocus and Red Line trenches), visited positions numbers 2 and 3. Number 3 being in the second line trench. Started to walk back over open ground, but owing to area straff had to retire to trenches. We watched eight-inch shells bursting in Lens. An interesting sight.

1st November

Gunners went down to waggon line. We all moved our beds to the signallers headquarters. A huge cellar, well equipped with beds. We had no intention of overworking - we cleaned the six guns, greased all the bright parts, and that was the job done. As to food, this was sent up every night, far more than we needed. Riddock was cook. Blackburn and I busied ourselves with our own dugouts. I made new beds (three tier) scrounged doors. These I fitted to the dugout and living room. At the same time constructing weird yet effective "locks" for these doors. Three visits we made to the reserve positions. Paying visits on each occasion to the front line

November 2

British Government issues the Balfour Declaration which supported the establishment in Palestine of a national home for Jewish people

November 6

Passchendaele was finally taken and Ypres relieved

November 7

Bolshevik Revolution in Russia results in Communist government under Lenin taking office

Britain captures Gaza under General Allenby

trenches. With field glasses, we spent several interesting hours at the Observation Point. No wonder that the O.P. Officers were keen on the sniping stunts.

8th November

Gunners returned. "E" sub were pleased with the improvements. Coppin was number one, Wringe was Sergeant Major. Beech having returned to his old Brigade. (The Guards) Several incidents which happened. Many a time did we get a bit of sport. Flocks of flying geese were common on this front. All in the vicinity would get out their rifles. I only remember one goose being hit, and this we did not get. In the churchyard in front was a tomb containing a well-preserved corpse. From the tombstone, we learned that it had been dead for nearly twenty years. Now this corpse I both saw down in the vault and on top of the ground. Down again and on top again...

20th November

Carting ammunition from the cemetery. Went down to canteen in the square. Blenkarn of "F" sub (an old Indian Soldier) was running a "crown and anchor" board. He was supposed to be up at the reserve positions. Was his daily task visiting the "reserves." Guess he never went further than the canteen. He "paid" for my silence on the

November 16

Clemenceau becomes French prime minister

November 20

British launch surprise tank attack at Cambrai

subject. Nearly hit when coming through square. At night a fight occurred between Coppin and Sergeant Rownie ("F" sub). Rather exciting.

21st November

Coppin went to wagon line and we were informed that we were to welcome a new sergeant. This being Sergeant Parkinson of "A" battery. As to what he was like, we wondered. If not "one of us" he would have to be brought round. But he turned out to be above our expectations. Same night, Douglas, taking a bath badly scalded his foot!

22nd November

I was detailed to take a course of fitting at an ordnance workshop. This news was pleasing. Went down that night riding with Corporal Tremmlet in the cooks cart. Back to Souchy. Wagon line – called on Wringe. He fixed me up with supper and bed.

23rd November

At 10 A left for Aix Noulette on horse, with driver to bring back horse. My new headquarters were with the 26th Light Canadian Mobile workshop. The men were having a half day. A football match. After tea, a walk to Bully Granay passing through Bully le Mines. Granay a large village. The lower part of the town was often under shell-fire. The high part had been hardly touched. The civilians taking no notice of the happenings. Coal mine in the village was still being worked. Although only three miles from the Trenches – very strange that villages behind were absolutely shattered, this village although a deal nearer had hardly been touched. Shells would howl over finding billets behind on the Arras main road and Gouy Servins - What gay times we had in Granay – Dancing, singing, Canadians came down from Vimy Ridge for "a drink".

24th November

Started work. Gun repairs. While there, slept in a tent - Beds – Three of us, one being an old South African soldier. He knew the game with regards to providing suppers.

25th November

Fitting tanks to guns, and testing sights. A 296 Battery gun came in badly smashed. These workshops were well equipped. Lathes, and emery wheels driven from lorry engine. Electric drills. Bully at night. A bit of fun in café. A party of civilians were at a café celebrating a wedding. All that. Sampled a few wines. One man with a huge walrus moustache was extra lively. We made him dance and sing. In the end, someone cut off one side of his huge drooping moustache. He was then sent home. A gay night

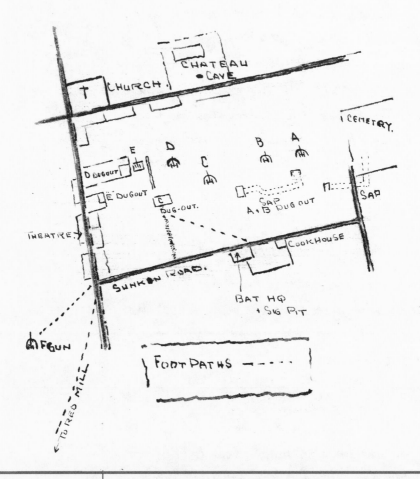

THE LEIVEN POSITION.

26th, 27th and 28th November.

In Workshop.

29th November

Putting up nissen hut. Afternoon I walked over to
Breiby. Searching for Brown of Barley. The 11th
Division signallers were stationed there. Failed to
find him. Baths. Spent evening in Y.M.C.A.

30th November

News came along that we were to return to battery. Was supposed to have remained at shop for three weeks, but the Brigade had had an urgent call. The Germans had broken through on the Cambrai front. A British offensive had been put up. The objective had been taken but troops advanced too far. No support.

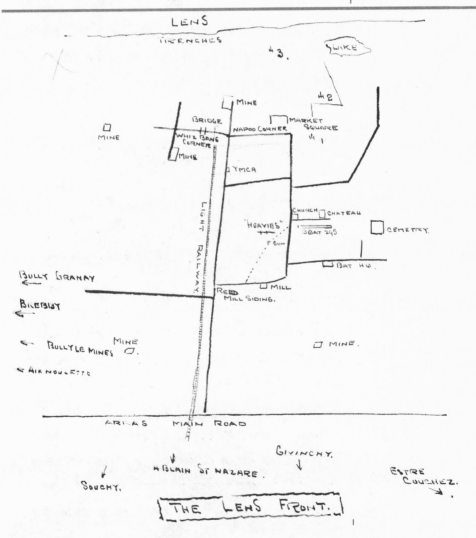

THE LENS FRONT.

The enemy had launched a counter attack and the British were worse off than before, so I with an "A" Battery Gunner packed up. Carried our kit. We had not much with us it is true, but it hung heavy before the journey was finished. We cut across country and at 4 p.m arrived at the souchy wagon line only to find that the Battery had departed. We were undecided whether we should shelter for the night, but decided to push on. Next day the battery would be on the move again. On making enquiries, we found that they had gone to Estree Cauchy.

BœTHUNE.

We remembered it by the words we often used "extra cushy". Something to do I believe, with sleep in the French lingo. We managed to get a lift in a wagon for a few kilometres. Again had to walk. We walked and walked. And out there, walking was not a pleasant occupation owing to the bad state of the roads. Arrived somewhere about 8 P.M. tired out. George Inkson made us

some supper. The boys had got me good sleeping
quarters (in tents). An hour in a wayside café
and then bed.

1st December

Packed up and off at 10 a.m, a nice day. Jogged
along. Gunners nearly always walking. Such weak
horses? And at 3 p.m, arrived at Arras. The old
town had seen its share of fighting but it was
not too badly smashed. There were still a few
civilians left. A few shops and estaminets. Put up
horse lines. Billeted in house exactly opposite the
main door of the cathedral. A very dark night.
Visited the B.E.F. (British Expeditionary Force)
Canteen. And went to a concert given by the
"Whizz Bangs" Concert party.

2nd December

When packing in the morning, a few long range
shells fell in Arras. Moved off 10.30 p.m. Rain.
First saw Captain Paton (of the laces fame) was
wagon line captain. If he had had charge of the
gun line, I hardly know where we should have
finished. Many a laugh we had over his strange
sayings – Here are some examples : Anderson was
Battery Barber. Paton "What are you doing
Anderson?" Anderson "Haircutting, sir". Paton
"Hay cutting! I can't see any hay". Another: A
gunner taking some milk to a sick comrade.

Paton "what are you doing?" Gunner "taking some milk to ----who is sick" Paton "Beer! Don't give him beer". And Paton, on seeing two men fighting said: "For ----- sake don't fight it's too ------- hot". In the late afternoon we arrived at Courcelles. Billeted in Barn. A small village, we retired early to bed. Very funny about these barn billets – Perhaps the barns were half full of straw – to look in, one would see candles burning everywhere amongst the straw. This was so. Still we never had a fire. Courcelles was within the sound of the guns and from time to time, a stray shell would fall in the village. We became better acquainted with the village in March 1918.

3rd December

Moved off through Bapaume. Badly smashed. Halted at Y.M.C.A. At 2.30 p.m, we arrived at the new wagon line. I remember I was driving in "the Wheel" at (the) time and knocked down a gatepost when entering field. Looked over guns. Village was Haplingcourt. Y.M.C.A. At 5 p.m left for the line through Metz and Metz Wood to Demmicourt. When a mile from position, the centre off horse of our gun fell, exhausted, suffering from an old wound received in the salient. Paton's first words were "where is my revolver?" He would have finished it off. (I suppose that the horse still lives) Jock, much to his displeasure, had to remain behind with horse. Was a beautiful night, but very cold. After dumping guns and unloading shell, we made a rough bed. A sharp frost.

4th December

A very open position on the site of some old German horse lines. Remains of dozens of small billets. Been pulled to pieces, but we did not take long to reconstruct one for our use. The village was 200 yards in front. Water pump to right. "C" and "D" had gun pits, we started building a sandbag wall around ours.

5th December

The frost gave – ground became soft. Unable to hold the trail spade. Spent most of the day searching for and making a suitable trail bed. Clark came up. Out billet was quite comfortable. Narrow – hardly enough room to stand up in. A stove we made out of an old oil drum. Chimney from a biscuit tin. At night it was real comfortable. As to the arrival of Clark; a man of about 46 - tall – had been an insurance agent in Birkenhead. We soon weighed him up –

A voice:
"Is this "E" sub?"
"Yes, who are you?"

"Gunner Clarke and I've been posted to "E" sub."
"Come in"

And in he came with a bundle of kit as long as himself.

"What is this?" said Parkinson
"My kit"
"Well take your ------- kit outside".

That quietened him down. He came in and of course he was cross-examined by us. Well as to what he knew, how long had he been out, etc., he had only just arrived out. That night we were on duty. This did not please Clark. All the next night we were firing. "When do we sleep?" inquired the newcomer. We named him "Mrs Clark", and the name stuck to him. A nice old fellow, but a week of roughing it would have killed him. We felt really sorry for him and arranged that while he was with us, he should never do guards or night duty. In return, he had to act as our servant. Collect wood, fetch water, sew on buttons, prepare our suppers – the arrangement pleased him and he looked after us well. And every night he slept. Can see him now. Always slept with his tin hat on.

December 7
US declares war on Austria-Hungary

8th December

British fell back 1500 yards. Unable to hold <u>Bourbon Wood</u>. The evacuation was a surprise to the Germans. When he was seen to occupy the wood, there was a concentration of artillery fire on the front. He must have had a warm reception. We had a good nights rest. We were surprised to see a fresh 4.2 shell hole outside our billet door when we rolled out in the morning. We had heard nothing. One could sleep.

DEMMICCURT.

8th – 11th December

Much of a sameness in the routine. Plenty of night firing.

12th December

Relieved by the 51st Division. Changed guns, and we "relieved" them of trench sheets and other useful articles that had been left unguarded. A general service wagon carried our kits and we marched. The roads were very bad, a misty morning. When passing through Roulescourt a plane loomed through the mist. Had no idea it was a German machine until it attacked an observation balloon, destroyed it and on returning, machine gunned our column. No one hurt. I had a bad foot. Had to fall out. After a

December 9
Jerusalem falls to Britain

December 10
Panama declares war against Austria and Hungary

December 12

Cuba declares war on Austria and Hungary

rest at Ribicourt followed on. Arrived at dusk at new position near Flesquieres near sugar refinery. Slept in a trench.

13th – 14th December

Not a bad position. Fired at close range. At night could hear the machine gun bullets whining over. The guns and pits were as left by the 51st. Position – Not a bad spot. Plenty of cover, and ammunition was brought up on a light railway. We were shelled frequently. Spare gunners went back to prepare new position. Walk down to Grand Revine for ammunition boxes. Found dead man in a shell hole.

15th December

December 15

Russia signs an armistice with Germany

Packed up. Shelled heavy. 5 p.m, teams came up. Retired to new position a mile in rear and remained there until 27th December. Daily routine had much of a sameness. The Germans didn't give us much rest. And we had several slight gas attacks. Quite mild ones, except for one on the 24th. The horses pulled guns as far as trench. By hand we pulled them over the ridge and down into the wood. All night we worked cutting down trees that were in the path of guns. By daybreak, all were in position with the exception of "F" sub. This gun slipped into the trench. Took half day to get it out.

As to position:
In a wood known as Triangle Wood (was the shape of a triangle), stood on top of a hill, forming to slope down to the Grand Revine, the latter being a broad valley. A light railway ran down the centre of valley. On our left front was Haveringcourt and the wood of the same name. In front of the wood ran the old Hindenburg Line trench, well made, ten feet deep. At one end was a sap, sleeping quarters of the officers. Rear of the wood was the signallers pit. A German plane lay in the wood. A good wall we built round the gun, and made a tree branch covering over all. In the trench, we made quite comfortable dugouts. Aiming posts were on hill at the back of wood. Some good times we had. Our sing songs and jazz bands. Rum was plentiful. Parkinson was acting Sergeant Major of the gun line. An infantry mess tin full each night for the five of us and then we would help "F" sub to drink theirs. Allen and Atkins hadn't a great liking for the "fire-water". Their dugout was opposite, and complaints they made because they couldn't sleep. I quite believe it. The front was also a big salient, but deeper than at Ypres. Front was known as the Cambrai Front.

This is an idea:

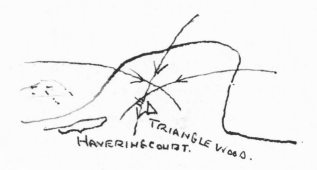

TRIANGLE WOOD.
HAVERINGCOURT.

Metz shells came from all directions, at night with the flashes all the way round, we used to wonder which way out.

December 22

Russia opens separate peace negotiations with Germany (Brest-Litovsk)

DUGOUT IN THE OLD HINDENBURG LINE (gun of F sub on top)

sharp frosts set in. Later in the month - a little snow

23rd December

Cook's cart stopped a direct hit

24th December

Germans made a big attack. S.O.S 3 a.m. sergeant Roney "F" sub wouldn't stop firing so that we couldn't get up the steps. (see above sketch). He being on S.O.S duty was already on gun. We never forgave him for it. We had to wander round the back of wood and were nearly five minutes late in firing. Had a proper barrage put on us. A warm two hours. "F" sub broke a trigger spring. Couldn't put it in. Came and asked me, Parkinson told them to --- ------! Gas shells fell like rain. An enjoyable Christmas Eve or rather the morning of Christmas Eve. "F" sub blown in. Our dump blown up. Two gassed. Clark was taken bad. All day we spent repairing damage. Had myself several gas burns. We had a walk to the railway line. Never have I seen so much damage wrought in such a short time. And the sickly smell of mustard hung round for several days getting in all our throats.

Christmas Day

Never fired all day. The Germans never rested – biscuits and bully for dinner. (was our usual while on the Cambrai Front). Whiskey we had from the Major (Major Mausley). Two tins of cigarettes from Holloway Guard. At night blizzard. Spent night in signallers pit with three infantry machine gunners who were attached to us.

26th December

On this day we had <u>our</u> Christmas Day. We were relieved to go to the wagon line. Jack Inman came up to take over from Parkinson. First time we had seen him since gassed at Ypres. Nice day, but walking bad with the snow. Needless to say, we stopped to have one at every available canteen. After nine miles, we arrived at the wagon line at.Bertincourt — as much beer as we wanted - good dinner, Roast beef and plum pudding. With the beer we had and the rum soaked pudding — well. Afternoon: Visit to B.E.F. canteen and to pals in "A" and "C" battery. Cinema in the old barn at night — went well prepared with a petrol can of beer and rum. We were supposed to have walked that nine miles back to the line. We were seeing that we would or could not do it. German planes bombed the village. Under the circumstances it troubled us but little. Slept well.

Was a good Christmas.

27th December

We returned to line. Didn't feel much like the walk. News of a move and that this next move would be to a rest. This was pleasing news. In an old dugout we stored all the ammunition.

28th December

A terrible cold day. Never have I known a colder.
Teams came up. Only one team "roughed." One
by one the guns were pulled down to road in
Havringcourt Wood. Roney found a bottle of rum.
We had a good drink. Jock and Ablett took
charge of it. We had to go back to find them
and the bottle. We waited in the wood for the
teams to come up. A blizzard started. It _did_ snow
– made up a fire in a hut – Jock was told to
guide teams into wood. He asked the Officer
Holloway "What horses?" Inquiries as to where the
rum had come from, no one knew. Hooked in –
many a time did the team fall.

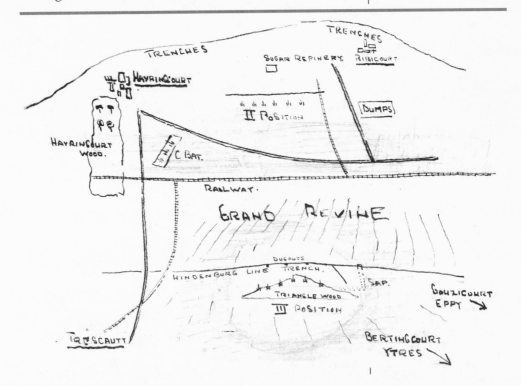

It was some journey. Jock and A. took some looking after. They got in an infantry ammunition wagon. Some one lifted the rear part up and they were tipped out in the snow. Horses going at the trot at the time. The fall brought them to their senses a bit. We strapped them onto the limber. At 2 a.m we arrived at <u>Bertincourt</u>. A good meal had been prepared for us.

29th December

Moved off – A nice day, but owing to snow, going was bad. A frost. Back to <u>Courcelles</u>, walked to canteen. Slept in huts near the railway embankment.

30th December

Moved off at 8 a.m. Nice day but cold. Arrived at our destination at 3 p.m. Where it was I do not know. Billet in French hut. Night in Estaminet. All merry and bright. Jock I remember was smoking a cigar. Jack Wringe took it from him. For days, Jock would say "I wonder who took my ------- cigar". We lost Jack Inman. Really this was a celebration of Jacks return. He had wandered down to "A" Battery, was in someone else's bed and refused to get out. Some night.

31st December

Moved off at 8 a.m. Passed through no big towns – through Ivergney, and the forest. – Leucheau (Lucheux) to Grouches Lucheau. A dreamy village. Guns and lines along the road. Billet in barn – Was not long before we found a coffee house – had a good supper.

And so ended the year 1917.

JANUARY 1ST 1918

Unpacked, washed down. Changed billet to better one – an old mill.

2nd January

Packed up again.

3rd January

Moved off at 10 a.m. Back through Leucheau and the forest to Ivergney. Re our stay in this village one can recall pleasant memories. Billet in large barn. Wire beds. Gun park and horse lines in front. At this place, I didn't do a single parade and never rolled out of bed until breakfast. Limber gunners had privileges. What with that and no guards... still in the line they were seldom relieved. Rough weather we had to

Timeline: 1918

This section lists the events of the year 1918, the final year of the war. This year saw the German military high command attempt one final large-scale offensive on the Western Front. A near success, Operation Michael's ultimate failure led to an increasingly sweeping series of successes by the Allies from the summer of 1918.

By the autumn the German Army was no longer able to continue fighting. With revolution imminent, Germany's political leadership petitioned for an armistice. It took effect at 11am on 11 November - the eleventh hour of the eleventh day of the eleventh month. The war was over, and with its end many of the European dynasties fell.

January - September

T.E. Lawrence leads Arab guerrillas in successful campaign against Turkish positions in Arabia and Palestine.

commence with. Deep snow, frosts, and then came the mud. In the mornings, a fire had to be lighted to thaw our boots. Impossible to get them (on) until they were thawed. A nice little estaminet was at end of gun park. It became known as the "Limber Gunners Retreat". I suppose that it merited the name. Several estaminets were made into club rooms for the boys. So cold in our barn that it was impossible to write a letter.

7th January

I had a day out. Went with a horse holder to buy cleaning material for the section, including a few odd tools. In early morning we started, taking food with us. Cross country to <u>Doullens</u>. A nice little town. Of course we deducted the beer allowance out of the money. A good day we had. The detachment thought that we were lost, or had sampled too much beer. It was dark when we arrived back.

8th January

January 8

Peace Proposal - US President Woodrow Wilson makes "Fourteen Points" speech to Congress and proposes the League of Nations

Training commenced for the divisional sports. I took part in the horseback wrestling practice, but was away on the day of the sports. Jock and Ablett that night burned down the guard tent. It was too ------- cold to live in a tent.

9th January

Four of us walked to Leucheau to divisional concert, taking a bottle of rum down to the Canadian Foresters. They paid us well. We could do with these extras.

10th – 12th January

I.O.M (Inspector, Ordnance and Munitions) inspection. My gun ordered for repairs. Tiffy Mackay was again my partner, and a good one too. Through Doullens, Jack Inman in charge, stopped at a café for dinner. On to Beauval via Villers Bocage (not new ground to me). (In fact it was the other way round. After Doullens, is Beauval and then on to Villers Bocage. They are on the National route 25 and the main road to Amiens) A good shop, but poor food. Still a good billet and while here we did not intend to work any more than we were forced.

Gun wanted relining. New springs and a tank fitted. In the shop also were three old gunners from 296 and 348. Norris Green and ----. He had an easy time. Spent most of time in coffee-houses. A dance hall we often frequented at nights. Whilst there, we "borrowed" two bicycles and went over to Frevent to see the people we used to visit when out at rest near Amiens. (This was a long cycle ride, back up past Doullens and up the D196 to Frevent)

January 19
Russian Assembly - A Constitutional Assembly in Petrograd is dispersed by Bolshevik forces

21st January

Went to boxing contest at Leuchean.

22nd January

Returned to battery. Blackler was in charge. The major had gone to England. The other officers to Paris. Had a reception from the detachment. A little celebration. Orders to pack up. I had a bad cold at the time. We were to go on a calibration trial. Just three drivers of each gun team and the detachments. Cold or no cold, I was going.

23rd January

Moved off through Leuchean, Authie, Sartau. Stayed the night in Louyencourt. To save me walking, I rode on a general service wagon. A comfortable billet we had in a barn at a farmhouse. The people were very good to us (and that is saying something). This village had been in the hands of the Germans for just one day in 1914. The(y) told us in quite good English how the Germans entered.

24th January

On again through Achean, Bouzencourt, Senlis, Albert to Meaulte. Quite a nice village, Y.M.C.A. at night. Billet in empty house.

25th January

Went on to the Fricourt range. The place is well-known to those th(at) took part in the 1916 Somme Battle. In the distance could be seen the well known landmark "The leaning Madonna of Albert". We were then only five kilos from Suzanne and Bray. What a change in the old battle field. Nature had almost obliterated all traces of war. We fired about thirty rounds each. Our gun was only two points above condemning. This report was pleasing, we had often been told that our shooting was erratic on the Cambrai Front. Seemed strange after such good reports while on the Lens Front.

26th January

We visited Albert in the afternoon. The town was badly smashed. Quite a number of civilians had returned. Quite a good time we had. The ruins of the Cathedral were most interesting. The Madonna still hung down. It was the saying that when the statue fell, the war would end - It was shot down in the March offensive – In Albert, was a shattered sewing machine factory - Piles of sewing machines.

27th January

Started on our return journey by the same route.

January 28

Invasion - Russian Bolshevik forces occupy Finnish capital of Helsinki

28th January

Arrived back at Ivergney having much enjoyed our trip, and the weather had been kind to us. Several little incidents I remember at Ivergney. Sergeant "Snooky" or "Snooks" (I never knew his proper name). A little fellow, everyone made fun of him. And always having his leg pulled. For all that, he was a real good worker – was Sergeant vet – When out at rest, he was much in demand for doctoring the horses and cattle of the civilians. We were all in the estaminet at the time when someone suggested having a joke on "Sergeant Snooks". A message was sent that the cat in the estaminet was "beaucou(p) malade". He came in with a rush saying "Madame, where is your sick cat?" We all pointed to the long neck china cat on the mantle shelf. The language was shocking.

On another date, a convoy of French wagons passed through Ivergny. One had trouble. Horse lost a shoe or something like that. We calmly watched the proceedings, wishing to "help" those in distress. We told the Frenchman that we could get them some tea at our cookhouse. Tea we obliged them with, but at the same time sorted out the goods on his wagon. Made a good haul, and covered it up as though nothing had

happened and our French friends went on their
way rejoicing. The "haul" was soon disposed of,
and the detachment was once more in funds. A
clever piece of work. One night Jack Inman called
me out of the estaminet. "Give me a hand to
take the nose bags off the horses." I helped him jes
off "A" battery's horses. Relieving the picquets.
We were always willing to help.

29th January

Cleaning up. Noticed a familiar face in the
park. A newcomer. I went down to speak to him.
Asked him where I had seen him before. Was
Gunner West of Arlesey. Had been a sergeant in
the "A" Battery of The Old Herts Brigade.
Warned for another "holiday". Next day was to
take my gun down to the Divisional Ammunition
Column at Milly. D.A.C. gunners and officers
were to use gun for instruction.

30th January

Packed my kit and joined the number one
Divisional Ammunition Column at Milly. Billet
in Barn.

31st January

Moved back to Gouches. Until 4th February I
remained there. A fine life, had the luck to be
billeted with an old pal of mine, Gunner Abery
(of Melbourn). It very much pleased him to meet

again someone from his own part and it pleased
me equally as much. An easy time I had, rising
at 9.30 a.m.

The type of
stove in all
french peasant
houses.   oven

THE FLOWER POT & COFFIN STOVE

Abery brought me my breakfast to me in bed –
at 10 a.m. Had to take the sights up to the gun
and bring them back at 4 p.m. During the day,
I passed the time with walks and made friends
with people at a farm outside village. We could
not converse much. Still we managed quite well.
Many an hour I sat with a book by the stove and
in the evening, Abery and I took trips to Doullens
to the cinema etc.

ALBERT

2nd February

Was a football match (cup tie: Divisional
Ammunition Column v Army Service Corps) at
Leucheau. Brown and Hudson were also with the
D.A.C. (from Hertford Heath)

4th February

Last I saw of Ted Abery. He was killed a few
weeks later. Left for the battery. Guns we parked
in the village street. Our rest was drawing to a
close.

5th February

Packed up. Our farewell concert. It was some
night I remember that I had the gloves on with a
little driver and I went down for the count.
Douglas had a busy time of it escorting us home.
Well it was the last day night for a lot of us.

6th February

At an early hour we left the village. A wet day.
Miserable on the road and in the late afternoon
we arrived at Bienvillers. This village too we
became better acquainted with at a later date.
In the distance we could hear the guns. Our billet
was in an old house near the church. Was the last
inhabited village in that sector. A few buildings
had been damaged either by shells or bombs. A
quiet evening we had. Visited a farm house.

Partook of supper. Girl at the farm had been wounded in early part of war. Turned in early.

7th February

Moved off at 8 a.m. Uninteresting country. Arrived at <u>Beugnies</u>. The wagon line (was) to be a village on the Arras Road. We were to relieve the third Division. Left our guns. Kits and belongings we tied onto the wagons and we moved off again, led by an officer of the 3rd division. At dusk, we arrived after passing through the sunken road. In the mud, the tools were thrown off (one of many pleasures).

Gun line in the village of Noriel. (Noreuil) Then 9 p.m made tea. We were shown our dugout. A cosy little place. We were informed that five men were killed in it only a week before – we began to wonder what sort of front it was – At the time it was quiet. In the night on S.O.S. A weak response. Could hardly believe that it was an S.O.S so different from those we had been used to.

8th February

Not much sleep. At daybreak we were about and the first thing was to make an inspection of the position and surroundings. Was a good position. If the Germans would have only behaved themselves we should have been A1. But it was not to be so. Only the centre and left sections at this position (four guns). The right section were in the valley behind (Death Valley)

The guns were in a line. Ground sloping to the right. The guns were dug into an artificial bank being chalk and clay dug from the sap in between "E" & "D" guns. A forty foot deep sap, two entries, and in this sap were billeted "C" and "D" detachments. I myself did not care for these saps. Too damp and not enough air. Even in dugouts a few feet below the ground had to be fitted with air excluding curtains. This being a blanket soaked with water and made to roll up outside. The pits were well made. Elephant iron and about five feet of earth on top. Racks for shells, and we greatly improved on our pit, fitting up our lighting apparatus, whitewashing, etc. The dugout was fitted with a two tier wire bed on each side. Our stove we erected near the doorway. Plenty of wood we had, and believe me in this dugout we spent some enjoyable evenings.

400 yards to the left was a light railway. We during our stay, constructed a railway line from the mainline to the main road. ("F" sub. gun). Then another line from there to "C" sub gun.

Plenty of work and we did our share of firing. The Germans were keen on area straffs. We didn't get a deal of peace.

February 11
US President Woodrow Wilson makes "Four Principles" speech to Congress

13th February

On guard, a rough night.

14th February

Another rough night. "F" sub were doing duty.
Was about midnight when bombardier Allen
came into the dugout and said that something
strange was happening. We left our cards and
went outside. A strange light then an explosion
then all was quiet. We returned to the dugout.
Half an hour later there was heavy shelling.
Cullen stumbled in nearly exhausted. GAS! We
rushed out to warn the others, all putting on gas
helmets except George Parkinson. Was rough. A
big cloud gas attack - That beautiful lilac smell
- we crawled over to the various dugouts. All the
time, our position was being heavily shelled. We
returned to the dugout satisfied that all were
warned, then noticed Parkinson's gas helmet. We
had to find him.

The saps were gas proof – thought that he would
be down there. The three of us were each to visit
different dugouts and pits and to meet again to
report – we met but had failed to find him.
Again we went out. Eventually found him lying
down by the cookhouse wall unable to move.
Luckily he had left his electric torch alight, had
this not have been so, we should never have seen

him. Three hours this attack lasted. Parkinson suffered no ill effects. Allen was bad. Had to go down.

15th February

Weather was improving. Major Montague in charge. Nearly always drunk. In spite of this fault, he was a clever man, conducted the work well and with the Brigadier General he was a great friend. Brigadier General Starling thought a deal more of him than our Major. Mausley was still in England. Nearly hit while fetching water.

16th February

Frost. Grand day. Two German planes brought down. A quiet day.

17th February

Nice day. Germans lively. Had to keep low all day.

18th February

Ablett went to right section as servant to Beddington. The mouth of the valley straffed with 5.9 (shells)

19th February

Dr. Shaw came up, and on this day the major in a speech told us of what we had to prepare

ourselves for. That the Germans would launch a
great offensive. I treated it as a sort of scare.
Bombardier Douglas took it seriously. "You may
laugh", he said. From that time onward we were
always arguing one against the other. He would
say: "If he makes an attack, who is going to stop
him?" I knew well that he (the German) would
get but little opposition. Really I didn't think the
attack would come off. Preparations to resist the
attack were then commenced. Hundredweights of
barb wire came up. Two machine guns. For
several days we were busy putting up barb wire
entanglements. Two rows round the position and
along the rail track. Emplacements were prepared
for the machine guns and firing trenches for the
spare members of the battery such as officers
servants etc.

20th February

Nearly hit while wiring.

21st and 22nd February

Wiring finished. Received instruction on the
Lewis guns. One afternoon we had a rat hunt.
Hundreds we killed using cordite in the holes.
Never have I seen so many rats. Many as huge as
cats and very tame too. In our dugout at night
when lights were out, there would be dozens. On
the beds and shelves, always had to sleep with

face buried under blankets. Have even caught them in snares. Pulling a cord when the rat's head was through the noose.

23rd February

Painting pit. Shelled heavy for two hours. Cookhouse and officer's dugout hit. No casualties.

24th February

Replacing wire that had been blown up.

25th February

Expected attack, but it never came off. Stood to day and night.

February 25

Rationing begins in London and the Home Counties

INTERIER OF DUGOUT NORIEL.

26th and 27th February

Lively days.

28th February

Shelled all day. A lid of a biscuit tin swaying in

the sunlight was cause of our cemetery being blown up. In the evening, went over and buried bones that had been blown out and erected the crosses again. Stuck them in just where we thought.

1st March

Shelled in afternoon. Walked back to rear section. This too was a good position. Pits side by side. Very near the slope of the valley. Sunken road other side of slope. Dugouts in bank. Ablett showed me all of interest.

One hundred yards to the left was the remains of a battery. Australian. From the crosses behind each gun one learned that nearly all had been killed. The foot of a dead German sticking through the bank, very much amused Ablett. Valley was about 300 yards wide. "Death Valley" and it well merited its name. The Germans simply poured shell in – big stuff too.

2nd – 3rd March

March 3

Russian Treaty - Soviet Russia concludes separate peace negotiations in treaty of Brest-Litovsk

Snow. Repairing entanglements. Plenty of firing. Spy "scare" saw an officer without hat strolling round our position. Spoke to no one. Douglas said that he must be a spy and followed him. Turned out to be "C" battery's Major. As you may imagine, Douglas was often reminded of his spy hunt.

5th March

Stood to all night.

6th March

Barrage at 4.30 a.m.

7th March

Stood to at 4.30 a.m. Aeroplane attack on German trenches. "F" sub went to hill on right front to act as tank gun. Very open position.

8th March

Ammunition up at 3 a.m. Brought up by Canadians on rail. Dumped by side of the main line. All in boxes. These we would load on our trolley and convey same as far as the road, about half a ton at a time. Many a time had we conveyed it that way but this night the brakes refused to act. Down the slope the lorry gathered speed. The brake was worked by the feet. Unable to jump clear owing to the barb wire. At the end of the line, the lorry overturned. The two of us riding, were thrown yards. Nothing worse than a few bruises. Shell boxes were smashed to atoms. Stood to at 4.45 a.m. A beautiful day. "Summer time" commenced.

9th March

Making main dump

March 7
Air raid on Kent, Essex, Hertfordshire and Bedfordshire. 23 people killed.

Peace signed between Germany and Finland

10th March

For the last two weeks, the spare gunners from the wagon line were kept busy constructing reserve positions. Digging pits and trenches and on this date, several of us went on the same stunt from battery. Was a beautiful day and the outing was enjoyable. Went past Vaux Vaucourt (Vaulx Vraucourt) and to left of Sugar refinery. At 4.30, we packed up and started for battery. Called at Y.M.C.A. in <u>Vaux</u>. Most of them returned via <u>Crucifix Corner</u> and the

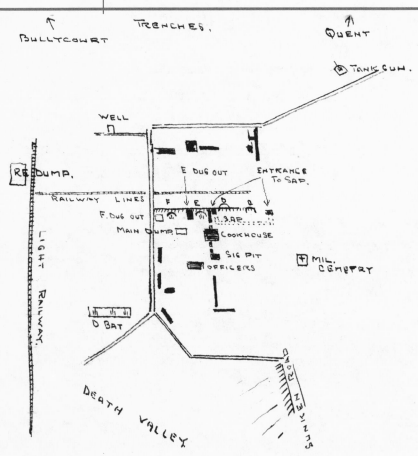

sunken road. Six of us decided to chance the valley. We wished that we hadn't when within a few hundred yards from right section, a German straff commenced. For an hour we lay in shell hole. Dare not show our heads above the ground. Officer's servant shook like a leaf. Thought he would develop shell shock. At night we raided the Royal Engineers dump to left. Parkinson keeping the sentry occupied.

11th March

Orders to move rear. Doug said "Now what about it?" This attack he could never forget. He had even told me that I should knock a hole through the cookhouse wall so that the gun could be blown up "if the worst came to the worst". Needless to say, his wishes were not complied with. At 8 p.m. we were pulled out. Left section only. Pulled back to open country. Not a position that had been already been prepared. All night we dug, and at daybreak, we stood to.

12th March

Still digging. Made a rough "bivi" in bank, three hundred yards in front of gun position. At end of valley on the north slope firing north, front formed a salient. To right was a German cemetery. On the hill in rear was <u>Vaux</u> – <u>Vaucourt</u>. To the left rear was the sugar refinery

March 12
German troops land in Finland

and waterpoint. In bottom of valley was the light railway.

13th March

Sandbagging walls of pit. Made dugout for signallers. Expecting attack. On guard alone all night

14th March

Digging pit lower. We're having the best of weather. Real springlike. The countryside fresh looking. Hardly a shell hole was visible. At night went up to the Y.M.C.A. at Vaux. Piano and sing-song.

15th March

Started making dugout for "F" sub behind gun. Brigadier General came up. He advised digging a trench from dumps to guns.

16th March

"F" sub dugout finished.

17th, 18th and 19th March

Digging trench only two foot deep. Started on our dugout.

20th March

Lengthening trench. In evening went up to Vaux. Had a good time. Gunner Goode (a newcomer) telling us how he had been in the Navy for a

year. Got in a supply of beer. At 10 P.M. arrived
back. All in "F" sub playing "Nap". All were
lively. Tremlett a rather sedate sort of person
(Corporal in charge of "F" sub) did not approve
of the gaiety. At midnight, the game ended
abruptly. Someone in our sub knocked out the
light, grabbed the "kitty" and we dashed off to
our dugout in front of the guns, Parkinson
getting hung up on some telegraph wires that
had been blown down. Settled down to sleep.

21st March

I called the others at 3 a.m. The Germans were
shelling the trenches more heavily than usual. I
went outside, but it quietened down. Again at
3.30 was another. Again I looked out. Some
remarks of course came from Parkinson about
people who can't get to sleep. At 4.30, the straff
started in earnest. Shells fell near us, an unusual
occurrence. Douglas and I made our way to the
guns and it was a good job too. Clarke was then
with us. Fired "counter preparation". S.O.S had
not then come through. The other two of them
then came over. S.O.S. We fired as quick as we
could get them in the breech. Clarke had his
first experience on the gun. He went completely
deaf. GAS! Daybreak. A misty morning, sun
breaking through at 8 a.m. Terrible was the
straff. Could even see our gun vibrating. Ordered

March 21

*Michael Offensive -
Germany launches
Spring push,
eventually mounting
five major offensives
against Allied forces,
starting with the
Battle of Picardy
against the British*

to carry on. 30 second fire; four fatigue men came up. They came up really to help digging the trench, but they were kept busy carting the ammunition for us. Lieutenant Wilson who was in charge had the "wind up". I remember him saying to Parkinson "where is there shelter? We shall all be killed" Parkinson replied "there is no cover, sir". Then Parkinson started joking. This I believe made Wilson worse. The barrage came within one hundred yards of guns in four occasions. A curtain of fire – the village of Vaux behind us was gradually disappearing. And then the curtain of fire came on. The ground was absolutely ploughed up. Wilson and Goode were killed, Ashcroft, Clarke, Tremlett and three others wounded.

MAR 21 1918.

The sandbag walls were hit, camouflage burned dumps blown up. Our dugout in the trench (or bank), blown up. We bandaged them as best we could. Ashcroft was in a proper mess. Arm just hanging on and was wounds from head to foot. A signaller we found head first down the signalling pit with a terrible wound in his back. We eventually got all wounded away.

Parkinson had previously been down towards the railway line and gathered a few scraps of information. Not much except that the enemy was rapidly advancing and that nothing could stop them. That the forward and central section of our battery had been captured, was then about 11 a.m. All communication lines had been blown up. So we were left to it. Parkinson informed us that there was nothing to do but to stick it to the finish and be careful with the shells.

At this time there were five of us left including Parkinson and the cook. Parkinson was joking about the whole occurrence. He at that time was wearing a brilliant red chamois leather waistcoat. He said "if the Germans capture me they will think that I am a ...... monkey", and many a reference to my birthday. (My birthday being on this particular day).

Douglas was as usual looking ahead. I really believe that he was pleased that the "day" had come, forever reminding me that his forecast had come true. "Now what about the hole in the wall" he would say. All the time we kept up a steady fire. Doug and I stuck in the pit. All at once we would quicken up. Ten rounds gunfire would bring Parkinson up "at the double" and this was his usual: "how many times have I told you to keep steady, you will want those shells". But it wasn't long before we had to be told again. Parkinson had been scrounging in Wilson's dugout. The chief spoil was half a bottle of whiskey. Very acceptable. All this time, the position was none too healthy. At 3 p.m. Lieutenant Scott who had escaped from forward position, joined us. From his appearance he had had a rough time. He wouldn't tell us what had happened to our chums. And later on: an infantry major came up, asked us where our officer was. Saying that it was disgraceful to let the enemy advance as they were. "Look behind you" he said. There were the Germans on the crest at other side of valley. We could hardly believe it. Not many hundred yards away. He asked us what we were firing at. Well we didn't really know. Rather a strange state of affairs you might think. But there we were on that hillside, had received no orders since the S.O.S Our signallers when the wires were cut went out to get news. They did not return. Either killed or wounded. All day we had been firing on the old S.O.S line. This being now miles behind the German front line. I guess that the Germans must have smiled.

We were then under machine gun fire from rear, and German planes machine gunned the position from a low altitude. The weather couldn't have been better. Such summerlike weather seems out of place. We were clad lightly. Most of our kit was in the trench "bivi", by this time, blown in.

Douglas was making preparations for the "Hun" appearing over the ridge. All rifles were loaded and had mapped out his retreat. Sure I do not think that his ideas would have materialised.

At 5 p.m we received our first order of the day. That was to drop our range from 5,000 yards to 500. This was impossible - live burst shells on the ground twenty yards in front of guns. At 6.30 p.m, the teams came up. Well none of us ever thought of ever being pulled out. In the meantime the infantry reserves had pushed the enemy over the hill in the rear. The guns were hauled out. Parkinson and I staying to bury Lieutenant Wilson and Goode.

Dragged them into a shell hole and covered them up. (I have often wondered if they were ever found again.) We walked back down to railway and along trench. Many wounded we saw - Fed up with it. Not caring whether they escaped or not. At Refinery Corner, we had to crawl in and at last joined the guns and we learned the truth as to the fate of the boys. 10

p.m we went back into action. Still without tunics and kit –

THE FATE OF THE OTHER SECTIONS

Noriel position

They were firing S.O.S Did not even know that the Germans had come over until they were seen in the ruins 100 yards in front. They were kept at bay for a while by the barb wire but eventually surrounded. Hair-raising tales were told by the survivors. With one gun alone ("C" sub had been blown up) They fired at fuse "o". Our old pit was blown up. "C" sub was blown in, burying two men, Coverdale being one of these men. They were already surrounded when Major Mausley ordered those still alive to dash for it. I believe only two returned. Last seen of the Major, was standing in the cookhouse passage with a shooter in each hand, with the end of the passage piled up with dead Germans. How Lieutenant Scott knocked several out with a shovel. The Major was wounded and captured. The valley position fared a similar fate. For a time, the guns held the mouth of Death Valley, but the enemy swarmed up into the sunken road and extended left leaving the valley clear. One described them as "a crowd going to a football match".

Newspaper report:

FOOTBALL TEAM OF SONS

Death of Father of Family of Eleven Who Played Another Side of Brothers

A novel football match is recalled by the death of Thomas Coverdale, retired farmer, of Hollym, near Withernsea, aged eighty, whose funeral on Saturday nine sons and three daughters attended.

Mr. Coverdale's eleven sons met eleven brothers named Charlesworth from Scunthorpe, Lincolnshire, on the Hull City ground in March, 1914.

Over 6,000 spectators saw that match, which was for charity and was won by the Coverdales by three goals to nil.

Two of the brothers were killed in the war.

(newspaper unidentified)

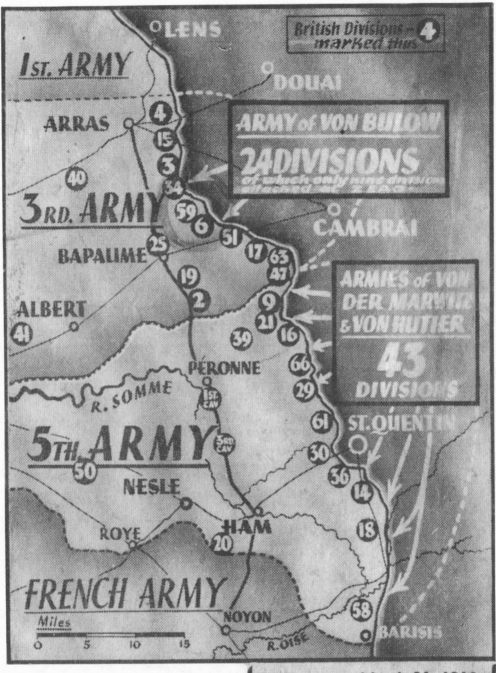

Battle scene, March 21, 1918.
Note weight of German
attack on Fifth Army

Bombardier Whitton mounted his machine gun in the sunken road, and exhausted his supply of ammunition. Said he must have killed hundreds of them. (Received the Military Medal). Guns were destroyed, and the remaining gunners retreated with rifles. The survivors were boasting how many Germans they had shot during the retreat. Several remaining (i.e. the gunners) with the infantry for some days. Gunner West was killed. They said that he kept them all alive. Was badly wounded and would go back himself, was hit by another shell when leaving the pits. Gill wounded. Ablett half carried him back.

LOSSES OF OUR BATTERY

4 guns   3 Machine guns   All kit
32 men out of 46 in the Line at the time.
Including these officers and N.C.Os

> Brigadier General Starling Gassed
> Colonel .... Killed
> Major Mausley Wounded and Prisoner
> Lieutenant Wilson Killed
> Lieutenant Godfrey Killed
> Sergeant Henstock Wounded
> Sergeant Coppin Wounded and Prisoner
> Staff Sergeant Scott Gassed
> Corporal Donaldson Killed
> Bombardier Blakey Killed
> Corporal Wormleighton Wounded

Corporal Bryson Killed

Bombardier Nuffield Wounded

Corporal Signalman....... Missing

Corporal Tremlett Wounded

Bombardier Whitton Gassed

Tiffy Macay Wounded, Missing. (died later)

Corporal Pay Clerk... Wounded, Prisoner

The remainder were gunners.

And this is how the Brigade fared:

A Battery Lost 2 Guns

B Battery Lost 4 Guns

C Battery Lost 6 Guns

D Battery Lost 6 guns

Only eleven guns remained in the 59th Division. The infantry, hardly a man returned from those in the line at the time and the reinforcements sent up suffered heavily. And at 10 p.m we were in the line again. A good rum issue to keep us alive. We were made up with spare gunners (wagon line officials). Doug went to "F" sub and I took charge of "E". Got into action and snatched a few hours sleep under the gun.

22nd March

Up at 4 a.m A good rum issue and the day commenced. Dawn came, fairly quiet. Germans had been busy getting their guns up. Position in open field left rear of Mory. 300 Yards in front

March 22
2nd Battle of the Somme - German troops reach the River Somme and capture Peronne

of Nissen Huts. The 11 guns of the Division in a line. The outlook did not look healthy. We partook of breakfast in the Nissen Huts. More ammunition came up. Sergeant Major Jack Wringe visited us. Brought us cigarettes and biscuits which he himself had supplied. And then a General came up. Informed us that it was up to us to stick to it and that reinforcements were on the way. 10 a.m. The fun commenced. The Nissen huts behind us went up like metal boxes, and we commenced S.O.S Amidst the heavy shelling, we worked like niggers. I do not know how we escaped being hit. Various guns and dumps fared badly in the line. 3 p.m. we were surprised to hear that the Germans were once more rapidly advancing. Rapid drops in range we had. And at last had to gallop out. The whining of bullets informed us that we had left none too early and we again saw his troops in conflict with the infantry. Major Ackermann of "A" Battery took two guns to crest and smashed a cavalry attack. In the valley we halted. Unable to fire as range was uncertain. Back again, we went to hill. Position at <u>Beugnies</u> on the main Arras Road. This being the wagon line while at Noriel position. Wagons just moving back. Had a word to some of the drivers. The shelling was getting hotter. Beddington went to crest, but no orders to fire. The rattle in front had quietened down. His

intentions were to cut off the supports arriving.
We started digging a trench. We heard a cry
from a hut in rear that a shell just dropped in.
We dragged out three men, one being Moy (an
old Essex Battalion Man) [he was killed next
day]. And then our position became a "little
Hell". Shelled with 5.9 and 8" shells. A heavy
battery lay in front of us. The teams were just
passing us and going to pull them back when
they were caught in this heavy shellfire. Men
and horses lay in a tangled mess. We went out
and released the horses, most of which galloped
off, and shells were still falling. Our battery
horses rescued the heavy battery. Really the whole
affair was like a cinema film only more exciting
and we had got used to it. An officer with
private's tunic put some rather enquiring
questions to Parkinson to which P. did not reply
too politely. If he wasn't a spy....well! Night came
on. We paid a visit to the Officers Club which
had stopped a few direct hits. Still burning. We
made a fair haul. At 10 p.m all was quiet,
hardly a shot being fired. Bomb dropped near —
We squeezed ourselves in the trench. Parkinson,
Inman and myself in together. Rather a tight
squeeze, but welcome were a few hours sleep.
During the shelling, Jack Inman made a daring
ride. He really was mad at times, absolutely
asked for it.

23rd March

March 23

*Independence -
State of Lithuania
declares
independence form
Russian rule*

At 3 A.M. we were awakened. "Pack up".
Rumours that the Germans had surrounded us.
You may be sure that we quickly packed up. So
uncertain was the rumour that mounted men
were sent out to see if all was clear. All was well.
Cross country. Day was then breaking, we met
new artillery brigades just coming in. We could
muster up a cheer for them. We knew then that
we were not alone. We pulled into position left of
Gommiecourt road in front. Aerodrome on left
front, Railway embankment in rear. Ground
sloped up gradually to hill, a mile in front. All
guns open sights on crest. We were waiting for the
signal. Sure, the Germans would have got a good
reception. We were disappointed. Germans had
closed in on Mory. We fired all day. How strange
everything seemed. Plenty of guns on the Front
now and horses were picqueted in rear of each
battery. More like a training camp. At night, a
message came up for me from Jack Wringe
saying that I had to come down. A man came
up in my place and also informed me that he
had a surprise in store for me. I went down by
cooks cart, to the wagon line at Douchy. Reported
to Wringe. He made a bed up for me with the
Quartermaster Sergeant. Surprise had to wait. I
slept on until 10 a.m.

24th March

Was awakened by Len Mason of Royston. Indeed a surprise. At dinner time, the wagon line moved forward to the railway bank, only 300 yards in rear of guns. I joined gun again. At 4 p.m the valley was shelled heavy. These forward wagon lines!

A stampede took place. Horses – hundreds of them, mad with fear galloping in all directions, sometimes tied together others dragging posts and ropes. Many were killed. We had to seek cover between the gun wheels. Luckily our horse lines were sheltered by the railway bank. A train came up with troops. When on the embankment, it was under observation. How it managed to get clear, I do not know. Barrage and S.O.S until 9 p.m and then quietness. All along, a deathlike stillness reigned. Not a shot. No lights, except for the various dump fires. Wild rumours quickly spread. The village Gommiecourt, 1/2 a mile to our right, was stated to have been captured. Even mounted men were posted to stop any infantry leaving the line. Things were in a muddle. At midnight we had the order to "hook in". We did, and back we went to Courcelles, also all other guns in the vicinity, "Heavies" too.

Put guns into position, and awaited orders. Then "pack up" again, and back to the position

we had just left a few hours before. As it
happened, there were no ill effects.. Still there
might have been. Had the enemy only known
that our infantry was left to his mercy. So
disorganised was everything, that the
whereabouts of the enemy were unknown and the
rumours were said to have been originated by
spies whose duty it was to create havoc, and
disarrange the British line. We received orders to
report at once any suspicious characters.
Daybreak.

25th March

At 6 a.m we moved back to rear of railway and
we fired until 10 a.m. We were all about dead
beat. Order came through that we were inactive
and could be spared. Exchanged our two guns
with "A" battery and we pulled out to be made
up. Back to Douchy. Halted for dinner then back
again. Through Adinfer. Many dead civilians in
the street. Civilians trekking back. Roads were
choked full of traffic. Unable to move either way,
this also being due to spies. Were informed later
that several were caught. At one place, we had to
wait for three hours. Halted by the side of a
brigade just going into action. They had just
come back from the "Last". Quite a contrast to
us, all their equipment was spotlessly clean. They
were very curious as to what had happened to us

the remains of B 295. A beautiful night,
through Bienvillars to Suastre. Guns in orchard,
slept in barn.

26th March

Scrounging a bit of kit. Overcoats, puttees, etc.
Infantry came by. Going into action without a
round of ammunition. We had to hand over half
of ours. Rumours again that German tanks could
be seen advancing in the distance. We got into
action. A false alarm. They were only a column
of French tractors. Moved back into Gaudiempre.
Not a civilian left. We made some raids you
may guess. Beer and wine was plentiful - Barrels
of beer in the street, and we took in a store of
wine, storing some in our shell baskets. Chickens
and rabbits... We washed the guns down and
then we lost ourselves for two days. Civilian bed.

March 26

*Allied Conference -
Doullens Agreement
gives General
Ferdinand Foch
"co-ordinating
authority" over the
Western Front*

March 26

*German Advance -
German forces
capture Albert &
Noyon and advance
toward Paris*

27th March.

Yorks and Lancs. band, Guards division came in.

March 27

*Germans halted at
River Scarpe*

28th March

29th March

Moved to Bienvillers. (Bienvillers au Bois) Wagon
line in chalk pit, 200 yards from the village.
New guns came in and we were made up to full
strength again. "A" Battery had had a

March 28

*French counter-
attack – counter-
offensive halts
Germans
throughout the
Somme region*

smashing near Courcelles. Douglas and I made a "bivi" in side of pit. Not a success.

30th March

Getting guns ready. These went up mostly manned by the reinforcements. The old gunners remaining back for a rest. How we discussed our exploits of the previous fortnight. Everything was plain to us. How the 59th Division had been sacrificed. Well, it had been so. The official report stated that we were outnumbered by 20 guns to 1. The attack had then been expected. We had made preparation with barb wire and reserve positions, but we had no support. The attack came and sure it was greater than expected. No one could hold against such great odds. Even then, there was no support. We fell back. The prepared positions were lost. The dumps of ammunition could not be used. All were lost. That being so, our ammunition was short.

Never had the line been so disorganised. Every available man, airforce, cooks, labour corps were all given rifles and they had to help to hold the line. Although many of them had not seen a rifle before, they did well, and after a severe struggle, the line was held.

31st March

Two wagon lines had been formed. The forward wagon line being 100 yards behind the guns. I rode up with Parkinson. Having to bring his horse back. Walked from forward wagon line to battery. Position in trench right front of Adinfer Wood. Shelled heavy. Sergeant Duncan killed. Signalman wounded.

2nd April

Lieutenant Scott killed

3rd April

Sergeant Roney. Lieutenant Blackler wounded. Douglas and I moved our "bivi" to top of cliff being too muddy and wet below. Wagon line shelled heavy. Wildsmith was captain in charge. Horses had to be taken away. The two of us on top of bank had no intention of moving unless we were blown out.

6th April

Ablett, Doug, Mason and I had some enjoyable nights down in Bienvillers. Some civilians still remained. The village was gradually getting less.

7th April

Went up line with ration cart. Road shelled heavy. Two horses killed in 'amo' wagon.

April 1

The British Flying Corps becomes the Royal Air Force

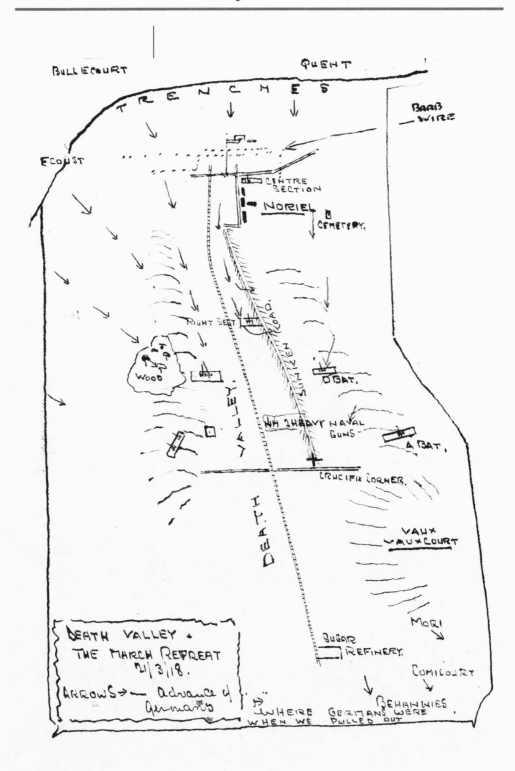

8th April

Wagon line shelled. Bit of shrapnel tore our "bivi" cover.

9th April

Bienvillers at night. In Estaminet. Shelled with 5.9 resulting in free beer. Ablett "wound up".

April 9
The Georgette Offensive – Germany launches second Spring offensive, the Battle of the Lys, in the British sector of Armentieres

14th April

Left for line at 2 a.m. Very dark and lively. Arrived at 4.30 a.m. Battery in action. Corporal Smith in charge of "E" sub. Then a new position amongst the shrubs rear of Kosmos Farm. Adinfer Wood on left. Adinfer Switch Trench in front. Douchy Road on right. A good trench, and old German gun pits. Golding and Corner the new Gunners of our detachment. Major Clark then O.C., (Officer Commanding). Best Major we ever had. Was a lively position continually being shelled. Plenty of firing.

April 14
New leader - Foch appointed Commander-in-Chief of Allied forces on Western Front

17th April

Moved guns 100 yards forward, our shrubbery being marked. Dug pits on side of hill.

21st April

Dug pit lower. Another attack expected. One of each detachment had to keep up each night. Dugouts. Ours was large. Too large to be safe. A fireplace in corner. The order was "if he shells, let

April 21
Manfred von Richthofen, the 'Red Baron', is shot down and killed over France

April 22 - 23
British Naval raid on Zeebrugge is huge success

us sleep" and so it was, but believe me, the one who was sitting up used to take cover in the trench. When asleep, one knew nothing. It was a wonder that the place was not hit.

25th April

Firing, no sleep. Shelled heavy for five hours. Pit hit and "bivi" missed by inches. Sergeant Pratt in little "bivi" with Sergeant Essex. "Bivi" blown in, Pratt wounded.

26th April

Building new wall to pit. Started digging "sap". Day and night. Work in shifts. Shelled heavy. Major Clark killed. Bombardier Ball wounded. Clark died while carrying him to aid post. Dull day. Shelled heavy. Medical Officer took shelter with us in trench. Lieutenant Allways and Lieutenant ..... drunk. Took shoot on our gun. I loaded for them. Shelled heavy at time.

Major Clark

30th April

Plane very low over battery. Thought we were in for it.

May 1
Western Front American troops join Allied Forces at Amiens

3rd May

Went to O.P (Observation Post) for iron. H.E (High Explosive) bursting over trenches. Jock and I with sheet of iron each. When near battery,

were shelled. Nearly hit. Had to lie in shell hole.
Crawled to trench. Shelled for three hours. Fired
all night.

4th May

At 7 a.m, a gas attack. For two hours the air
was thick but to our battery, no ill effects. "C"
Battery were unlucky. Their guns were in a
hollow. Was quite misty where they were. The gas
did not rise, but when the mist cleared it
evaporated slowly and by night all were gassed.

5th May

Rain, right and centre sections moved to rear.
Scrounging iron.

May 5
Germany occupy
Sebastopol

6th May

4 a.m, preparing position at right of road for our
left section. Sure it was time that we moved. The
position was getting too "hot". When removing
iron from Officers dugout, we were spotted by a
balloon (what "eyes" they had). Best shooting I
have ever seen. Near enough a direct hit with a
high velocity shell. This being a three inch shell
fired from an extra long barrelled gun resulting
in greater speed. Rather peculiar these shells, as
one had no warning.

6th – 7th May

This was the order:

1. You see the shell burst
2. Hear it coming
3. Hear it burst
4. Hear the gunfire.

With the above order the shell would burst twenty yards to rear.

This particular shell missed us by about six feet. We did not wait for the next. At 9 p.m. We moved over to new position. Until 2 a.m we worked. Was raining. We crawled into the little "bivi" that we had made and were soon asleep. Called out at 8 A.M. Blankets soaked. A nice morning. Spent the day concealing position. Fired all night.

Position on slope : Adinfer switch trench in front. Douchy Road 100 yards to left. Left front Kosmos Farm. To right: Wood. The enemy did not give us much peace. Very little firing we did in day time. We did our share at night. We started on another sap. Two entries commenced at the same time. Day and night work. Only room for one man working at a time and one holding bag for filling.

8th May

Out with Mick Golding. Searching for "Mining sets". (Wooden pit props for reinforcing the walls and roofs of tunnels) Golding was an "Eastender" of the boxing ring type. Was never happy unless on the scrounge. We both excelled in this calling. If anything was required, we were sent out together. His pre-war history perhaps was not of the best. He showed me newspaper reports relating how he just managed to scrape off a manslaughter charge. Accused of pushing a man out of a railway carriage. But with all those faults there was not a straighter man in B295. For ever volunteering. If a man was sick on another gun, apart from our detachment, he would do his "shoot". He has said to me: "You look tired, have a sleep". I would refuse, but he would insist on having his own way.

9th May

Went to wagon line with Allen for bath and a new suit. Was to be a days holiday. Got up late, walked across country, visited main position. To Monchy. Lorry ride to Pornemie (Pommier) across country to St. Amond wagon line. Allen and I checked our new gun stores. Walked to Souastre for baths. Canteen. Rode back to gun line on limbers. Fired 9-3 a.m. Two of us would take it (in) turns to "stand to" each morning. There was always plenty of work for us clearing up after the night shoot. Empty cases to be removed and hidden. Replacing camouflage, covering up "Blast Mark" was very difficult. The problem of concealment at this position. The hillside was yellow with buttercups. Was difficult to match our camouflage with the surrounding countryside. At daybreak the enemy observation planes were busy. They would fly at a very low altitude. Those who were standing to were always waiting for them. Would get busy with the Lewis Guns. All batteries in the vicinity would be at the same occupation. Although none were shot down, they did not get much of an opportunity to look around.

11th May

Golding and I had a trip out up to "purple line trench". Open country in front. Could look down on the German line. Found a store of blankets. These were acceptable. Called in at Kosmos Farm. Guards had reserve billets here. Stayed to tea. Fired all night.

12th May

Inman, Golding and I went out. We had received news that the Royal Engineers had been digging out mining sets. These we found in a stack, in front of the "purple line". One by one, we carried

May 11

Peace signed in Berlin between Finland and Turkey

them and hid them under a bridge. On several
occasions we had to seek shelter. The visibility was
excellent. On our left ten miles away, we could
see Monchy le Pru. (Monchy le Preux) All our sets
were hidden and left on with "THAN Q" chalked
on it. At dusk, we collected the sets with a
general service wagon. Tanks came up.

14th May

Golding and I went to get some iron hoping that
we had spotted the previous day. Caught in heavy
straff. Had to shelter nearly two hours. On
arriving back, Lieutenant Beddington informed
us that he had been watching us, saying that we
would venture out once too often.

15th May

We had already heard that Halcombe had
returned to the battery as Major. He had left us
at Cambridge Road, Ypres, with the higher rank.
He was at the wagon line making things rather
warm. The gunners at the line were not pleased
with news. They did not know him. I knew that
for the drivers he never had much love. And as to
gunners, only four originals left. This day we
received news that Halcombe was coming up.

The officers were worried. Everything had to be
just so. Lieutenant Johnson was in charge of our
section. A good fellow. He also had the wind up

about the arrival of the new major. Halcombe arrived. His first words to me were: "What, aren't you ---- ---dead yet?" We sat on the gun seat talking for an hour or more. In afternoon, were shelled heavy. Golding and I were resting in the pit. Stuck it as long as we could. Finally had to retire to trench.

C Battery lower down trench, had two killed. Mason came up to take records.

16th May

shelled heavy. Gun nearly hit. sandbag wall blown down. C Battery 3 wounded, 2 killed.

We went down to help them. Golding and I received visit from our two "Guard Friends" They wished to fire a gun. They stayed until the evening shoots commenced. Their endeavours to fire the gun were amusing.

17th May

still on sap. This was deep enough now for shelter, but for my part I did not like them. (I once saw some men digging their pals out of a sap. The mouth of the sap had been blown in, ten men had been buried alive and were dead before they could be reached.)

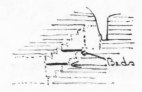

several gunners had made their sleeping quarters in this sap.

During night shoot, put "wind up" an infantry platoon returning from line. They would make a track in front of our guns. We saw that they were safe, and opened fire. They were then a few yards to the left of muzzle. The officer in charge nearly bubbled over with rage. I was to be reported, etc. He however realised that he had no business there. I reported it the next morning. The incident pleased them. We had sure had enough trouble in concealing their tracks.

19th May

Quieter day. I was relieved by Jock. Allen and I returned to wagon line. Slept in stores.

20th May

Bad luck at the gun line. Signalman wounded, Gunner York killed.

Great news. Brigade being relieved fourteen days rest. 62 Division relieving. Gunners came down. Rather upset with the bad luck that had occurred. Coldstream Band playing in village.

21st May

Packed up. Moved back to St. Leger.
Put up "bivi".

24th May

Moved back to Henu. Rain. Gun park on hill a mile from horse line. Slept in tent in valley at wagon line. Bombed.

24th and 25th May

4 A.M. twelve horses killed, nine wounded. Were all asleep at the time. One tent had its pole cut through twelve inches from the ground. Cut as clean as though with a saw and yet no man hurt. Not a thankful job cleaning up the mess in the horse lines.

25th May

Clearing up guns. Moved horse lines further up the valley. Warned for holiday by the sea. I could do with it. I had never felt so ill. Gathered a new kit together with the help of Wringe and Charlie Peters of "A" Battery. At end of the valley were the 42 Division Artillery, the section that had been with us at Vaux (Amiens). They too had fared badly.

May 24
Landings - British troops land at port of Murmansk, Russia

May 25
German U-boats appear in US waters for first time

Costa Rica declares war on Germany

LEWIS GUNNERS

26th May

Packed up and with Riddock left on horseback for Wallingcourt (Warlingcourt) Station. In first class carriage. Made ourselves comfortable.

27th May

At 6 A.M. arrived at Saint Valery. A rest camp on the cliffs. 1600 troops from the third Army. A holiday camp. Not a single parade. Best of food – amusements – arranged concert parties – sing songs – singing lessons – French lessons – YMCA – reading and games. A band playing every afternoon and evening attached to 37 Division.

Address being:

3rd Army Rest Camp
A.P.O. 5/59 –

Village (or town) St Valery three Kilos away. A small harbour at the mouth of the Somme. Several air raids in two nights. Had to take our beds to the beach. Le Houdell opposite side of the bay. Walked over one morning. Heard of German second push. This being below Amiens. Yanks had experienced gunfire for the first time.

5th June

General Byng visited camp. No parade, he visited every tent, speaking to all. I was feeling worse.

May 27
The Blucher Offensive – Third German Spring offensive – Third Battle of the Aisne begins in French sector along Chemin des Dames

May 28
US forces (28th Regiment of 1st Division) victorious in first major action, Battle of Cantigny

May 29
French Retreat French Forces driven back across River Aisne by German troops and Germans capture Soissons

May 30
Allied Retreat - German troops reach River Marne

June 6

US 3rd Division captures Bouresches and southern part of Belleau Wood

June 9

The Gneisenau Offensive – Germans launch fourth Spring offensive, Battle of the Matz, in French sector between Noyan and Montdider, near Compiegne, which is halted by the Allies

June 15

Italians prevail against Austro-Hungarian forces at Battle of Piave

sleeping nearly all day and voice bad with gas. That night went to sleep and on the 7th woke up in the 3rd Australian Hospital at Abberville (Abbeville)

17th June

Allowed to get up first time. Had been air raids every night. Ward a marquee with double walls. All who were fit to move had to retreat to underground dugouts during raids. Others had their beds lowered to the floor. The sisters stuck it well. During the raids they would wander from bed to bed. Sit talking to those who suffered with shattered nerves. Some of the lads in the ward with me were complete wrecks. Bombs dropped near enough to be unpleasant. One at the gate of our hospital. In the WAAC's camp were casualties. Chinese Labour Corps had several killed. Two bombs fell on the South African Hospital. Abberville itself suffered badly too. Great petrol dump was hit one night. Blazed for several days. It was an every night occurrence. Every night we waited for the signal gun and then would wait for the drone of the "Gothas". At sunset a ring of observation balloons would go up at intervals of 500 yards. Why? And what were they for? We did not know. Several planes were brought down. I was well looked after. Was kept busy when I could get about. Two bottles of stout each day was included in my ration. Otherwise lived on milk and the products of milk. A Y.M.C.A. in the grounds, a concert every afternoon.

Concert Parties:

Lena Ashwells
Rough Riders
The Diggers
Vet Band and Concert Party
Records

One of my jobs was to re-number books in the hospital library. Miss Birdwood was in charge of this section. (Daughter of General Birdwood of the 5th Army) When on that job was provided with "posh" teas. Then was moved over to A Block.

24th June

Was found a light job. This was in the operating theatre, wheeling the patients in, holding them down, and cleaning instruments after the operations. Some rather creepy experiences such as the removal of arms, legs, etc.

4th July

Marked out for Con (Convalescence) Camp; This being at Cayeux sur Mer. Felt better, but far from well.

5th July

Borrowed clothes and went with one of the operating theatre orderlies down to Abberville.

6th July

July 6
*US President
Woodrow Wilson
agrees to US
intervention in
Siberia*

Left at 10 A.M by Charabanc for the number 5 Con Camp. Twenty-two miles, passed through St Valery. Tents on the sand. Pine woods, and idea(l) holiday camp. Took the tip of an old hand, apply for work on arrival. That would mean six weeks at the camp. This I did. Obtained a job in the Mess Room. This work I commenced 15th July. A good job just to clear tables and sweep up. Only about three hours a day in all. No one was worked hard, and we had to get out and take walks. There were plenty of hostels and recreation rooms such as:

The Y.M.C.A.
S.A. Hut (Salvation Army)
C.A.Hut (Church Army)
R.C. Hut (Roman Catholic)
Scottish Church Hut.
Canteens
Cinema

Sea was 3 minutes walk. Cayeux was half hours walk. In between camp and Cayeux was New Brighton At the latter were several children's homes, homes for crippled children etc. Several large boarding houses on the sea front. These had been neglected. Up to the roofs with sand drifts. Several naval guns in turrets on the promenade. Was very seldom that we left the camp except for walks through the wood to the shore. A little estaminet we frequented in <u>New Brighton</u>.

13th July

Boxing contest. Five knockouts, exhibition by Paddy McAllister (Irish Welterweight).

14th July

Civilian Fete day at Cayeux. Lively day.

21st July

Sandstorm.

27th July

Walk to St Valery and Sallonelle.

14th August

Medical inspection. Marked fit. It had been a pleasant holiday. Had some good Pals. A Mourie (Maori) for one. This Mourie, the Mess Corporal and I ran a "Housy Housy" school (Bingo) at week ends.

Well - the corporal ran it and he paid us for our help.

July 15

2nd Battle of the Marne - Final phase of great German Spring push, British counter-attack

July 16 - 17

Assassination Former Tsar Nicholas II, his wife, and children, are murdered by the Bolsheviks

July 18

Final Allied Western Front Offensive Allies counter-attack against German forces, with positions along whole of the Western Front, seizing initiative

August 3

Russian Front Allied intervention begins at Vladivostok

August 3 - September 3

2nd Battle of Somme British troops mount massive attack. Germans suffer heavy losses of over 100,000

August 6 - 12

2nd Battle of Amiens Allies attack along a 15-mile front against German lines armed with 2000 guns and 200 tanks

August 8
General Haig directs start of successful Amiens offensive, forcing all German troops back to the Hindenburg Line; Ludendorff calls it a "black day" for German army

August 9 - 16
French Victory - French troops advance and capture Lassigny

August 11
German decision to end the war German General Ludendorff offers his resignation. The Kaiser refuses it but decides the war must be ended

August 16
Russian Front - Japanese troops land at Vladivostok

August 17
Russian Front - American troops land at Vladivostok

August 17 - 20
Battle of the Aisne French troops attack the Aisne Heights and repel the German forces

August 21 - 23
Battle of Bapaume The British recapture Albert, Bapaume and Peronne

16th August

Left Con. Camp at 4 P.M. Bus to Cayeux Station. Civilian train to Noyelles. Troop train through Rouen to Harfleur, the artillery base, arriving 3 P.M.

17th August

Through town to depot, stayed the night in Number 11 Casuals. Met about a dozen of the old 295 Boys and again we started soldiering, or were supposed to. Although I didn't do much and didn't intend to. Too many officers and N.C.Os who had never and never would hear a gun fire.

20th August

Went up the Pimple. A tremendous hill sloping up from the camp. All the training grounds were on the top of the hill. Had to pass gas tests (as if we hadn't experienced enough gas).

21st August

Up the Pimple again. My last trip up. Passed gunnery test, and at the base I remained waiting my turn for leave until September 26th. It didn't worry me. Only fatigues to do.
Found some quite good chums and needless to say "we played our cards right". Real old soldiers, not being seen much, so we were never missed. Plenty of amusements in the valley.

Numerous YMCAs, canteens, (and) a cinema holding 4,000 in our camp. So every evening, it was either a concert or cinema.

Concert parties at Harve (Le Havre):

Sons of Guns

Miss Johnsons

Yellow Dandies

Lena Ashwells

St Leonards

Scamps

Australs.

Mr Roberts M.P. gave speech in cinema.

15th September

Church service. Preacher Lena Ashwell. Other Church services by Kennedy (Woodbine Willy), Miss Booth (Salvation Army) and Higgins (Salvation Army).

Met several of the old lads who were wounded on March 21st. Had some good old times together. Boxing Contests, saw Bandsman Blake box.

26th September

5 p.m. Parade for leave. Marched five miles to Le Harve. Waited at station and in and out of estaminets until 11 p.m. Entrained. A lively crowd.

August 25

Battle of Grevillers – New Zealand forces capture Grevillers

August 26

Battle of the Scarpe. British troops capture Monch-le-Preux and break through the Drocourt- Quenat line

Sept 2 - 8

Battle of St.Quentin British, French & American troops attack simultaneously along a 12-mile front, cross the St. Quentin canal and capture Bellecourt

Sept 3 - 9

German retreat - German troops fall back to strongly fortified Hindenburg Line in an organized retreat

Sept 4

British Victories - British troops seize control of Canal du Nord and re-take Ploegsteert ('Plugstreet,), Bailleul, Kemmel and Neuve Chappelle. French Victory - French troops re-take Soissons

Sept 6

US Victory American troops advance to the River Aisne

September 12 - 13

US forces clear the St. Mihiel Salient, during which the greatest air assault of the war is launched by the US

September 14

German Retreat German troops retreat to the area between the Rivers Meuse and Moselle

September 15

Allies defeat Bulgaria – Allied troops break through enemy lines in Bulgaria and advance. Start of British offensive in Palestine, the Battle of Megiddo, and the capture of Syrian capital Damascus, defeating the Turkish Army

September 28 - October 22

2nd Battle of Cambrai – British troops attack German lines on 30-mile front from St. Quentin to Le Sensee

September 26

Battle of the Vardar pits Serb, Czech, Italian, French and British forces against Bulgarian forces

27th September

Arrived Rouen at 10 a.m. Marched to rest camp by river. Breakfast. Walk in City. Needless to say we enjoyed ourselves. Entrained again at 4.30 p.m.

28th September

Arrived at Bourlonge (Boulogne), "Coppins Rest Billet". Embarked at 3 p.m. Two hours trip. Sea calm. Folkestone. Arrived Waterloo 8 p.m. Stayed night at Kings Cross Hostel. .

11th October

Left Royston 8 p.m. Victoria Station by car to Buckingham Palace Hostel.

12th October

Up at 4.30. Train left at 6.30 a.m. Dover. Up to camp by castle. A long climb. Had a stroll round town. Embarked 3 p.m, arriving Bourlonge 5.30. During march up to St. Martins camp, two of us broke away from party. Spent evening in town. Later presenting ourselves at St. Martins. Slept in huts.

13th October

Moved to tents. Amused by a preacher in a YMCA or Salvation Army Hut converting some of the young soldiers. Mere boys being drafts to some regiment in the line. Many of them had perhaps only experienced a few weeks of army life. This parson was putting it a trifle too stiff, frightening the lads. These lads were awfully curious as to what they were going to. A little group put many questions to me. One couldn't help feeling sorry for them.

14th October

Paraded 10 a.m. Marched six kilos to station. Entrained 3 p.m. Down past Etaples.

15th October

Arrived at Harfleur Haute 1 p.m. Warned for draft.

17th October

Inspections. Off to the line again, and not sorry except we were bound for the Ypres salient. Most of us had been there before. A five hours march with full kit. Entrained 4 p.m. Our first exploit was to raid a wagon filled with apples.

18th October

Through St Pol. Bushy, Hazelbrooke, Brielly to St Omer. Arriving 2 p.m. March to Tilques. (2nd Army reinforcement camp). Cinema at night.

19th October

Slept in tents. A small village. Inspection and march past. Down to St Omer in afternoon.

September 26 - 28

Meuse-Argonne offensive opens; the final Franco-American offensive of the war. Fierce fighting forces the Germans to evacuate

September 27 - October 17

General Haig's forces storm the Hindenburg Line, breaking through at several points

September 28 - October 22

Battle of Flanders. British troops attack and reach Menin. They liberate Roulers, Capture Menin, Douai and Lille

September 29 - 30

Bulgaria concludes armistice negotiations with the Allies

September 29

Germany seeks an armistice. Commander-in-Chief Hindenburg and Quartermaster-General Ludendorff suggest that Germany becomes a constitutional monarchy and seeks armistice with the Allies to end the war

September 30

German Chancellor Count George Hertling resigns

September 28 - October 14

Belgian troops attack at Ypres

October 1

French Victory French troops capture St.Quentin

October 3 - 4

Germany and Austria send peace notes to US President Woodrow Wilson requesting an armistice

October 3

Allied Victory - Allied troops storm the Hindenburg Line and breach it, causing the Germans to retreat. Many German prisoners taken

October 5

French Attack. French troops attack along the Aisne river, crossing it on October 16

October 6-12

2nd Battle of Le Cateau

October 8

British Victory British troops capture Cambrai

October 10

British Victory British troops capture Le Cateau

Heard that we were bound for the 9th Division. About the exploits of this division, we had already heard.

20th October

March to town. Baths at old barracks. Lewis gun instruction. Concert by "Hanger Concert Party".

22nd October

Entrained at St. Omer. Through Hazelbrook, POP, old scenes that were familiar. Several thrown out of train. On to Meningham siding. Proven. Billet in huts with French soldiers in Estaminet.

23rd October

Marched off again 8 a.m. Through POP, Brandok, old wagon line, Flamertinge, (passed Dirty Bucket Camp). To 9th Division rest place near Marsh Farm, near Salvation Corner. In huts. Walk to Flamertinge at night.

24th October

Set off in open trucks through Ypres. Quiet now. The line was miles ahead. Was interesting to traverse again the old battlefield. Old guns. Destruction on Pilcom Ridge. When passing Weilty (Weiltje), could see site of old position. Tanks, dead Germans and at last arrived at Menin countryside unmarred. Marched to Winkel St.

Eloi. Arrived Harelbeke. Decent village. Billet in school that had been German Hospital, and so we joined the "Fighting 9th".

25th October

Bridges had always blown down. Civilians made a fuss of us. March to Am Col. Breakfast. From there to Battery wagon line. Dinner. We enquired from drivers what was happening and what was likely to happen. From the information received, the Ninth had started off from Pass(chendaele) Ridge. The German defence collapsed and the British just walked over. 200 Guns were captured on the first day, and from that date the advance had been gradual and sure. With the British advance, the civilians were coming back, returning to their homes in the rear of the advance. Some pitiful sights. Some civilians refused to leave. Many were killed. You may be sure that the troops were doing well. Fowl, rabbits and flour were plentiful. Billet in estaminet. At night, shells dropped round house. Gate blown down and chimney fell through the roof.

26th October

Joined Battery. Gun line went up as working party to construct pontoon bridge across a canal. A lively time we had. Several of the party killed. Higher up, a party of "Jocks" had been also

October 12

Peace Terms - German and Austrian-Hungary agree to U.S.President Wilson's terms that their troops should retreat to their own territories before any armistice is signed

October 17

Belgian Victories - Belgian troops enter the Belgian port of Ostend and also liberate port of Zeebrugge and town of Bruges

October 17

The new Czecho-Slovakian Republic is declared in Prague

October 18

Liberation of Lille Irish troops liberate Lille

October 17 - November 11

British advance to the Sambre and Schledt rivers, taking many German prisoners

October 21

Germany ceases unrestricted submarine warfare

October 21 - 31

Battle of Verdun American troops take part in fierce fighting

October 21 - 31

Battle of the Meuse
French troops in
action along the
River Meuse

October 24 - 31

3rd Battle of the
Piave –
British troops fight
with Italians at Piave
on Italian Front

October 25 - 30

Surrender in the
Middle East.
Turkish Army
surrenders to British
troops in
Mesopotamia

October 27

Erich Ludendorff
resigns

October 27

Peace moves -
Austria-Hungary
seeks armistice
through USA

October 28

German sailors
mutiny in the port of
Kiel

October 31

Revolution in
Vienna. Austrian
soldiers ask for
armistice

constructing bridge. These men had been provided with life saving collars. Had been working in the water. They must have had a rough time. Many had been killed. Was here while at work on this bridge I saw one of the most ghastly sights I had seen during the war. These men had floated down (dead) to our bridge. A group of about fifty heads supported by life saving collars and the moonlight on these faces...

Was pleased when the job was finished.

27th October

Crossed canal. Position near Vitchi. (Vichte). In turnip field. Fairly quiet

29th October

Many batteries pulling in. Position on left reserved for 281 Brigade Royal Field Artillery. Slept in cottage in rear. Civilian beds. The owner still remained. I well remember killing his fowls, cooking them and inviting him to supper. Ammunition up. A lively night.

30th October

On again, a new position.

31st October

Shoot 1 to 4 a.m. Jocks went over. Shelled at first, but it soon quietened down. On again at 9 a.m. On at gallop. Fired upon sites at machine gun nest. Two horses hit by bullets. 100 prisoners captured. On again, many dead in fields. Civilians coming past guns. Gallop through village that was being shelled heavy. We kept low on the limbers. "F" sub gun came unhooked and they left it behind in village . Strange that they did not know that it was missing. Through the shellfire they again had to pass.

1st November

Position between two windmills. Very lively. No one hurt. Took some souvenirs off some dead Germans. Did not fire much. Pulled out at night. A rough trip. Narrow roads, many wagons went into ditches. Numerous fires in district. Went back to near Stokerley Catherine (Stokerli Ste. Katerina).

2nd November

Nearly hit by bomb when at canteen.

4th November

March Past near Hulste by King and Queen of the Belgians. Jocks massed bands. Were informed that in a few days it was likely that the war would end. If no armistice, we would carry on. We should take part in a great "Push", and from the stuff that was coming up in support, we fully realised that it would be some push. Tanks, both

November 1 - 11

Battle of the Bourgogne – American troops advance through the forest of Bourgogne

Battle of the Sambre – British troops advance from the River Sambre to the River Scheldt

British Victory – British troops clear Le Foret Mormal and capture Valenciennes

November 3

Trieste falls to the Allies; Austria-Hungary concludes an armistice

November 4

General cessation of hostilities End of armed hostilities between Austria-Hungary and the Allies Civil revolution in Hamburg

November 6

*French & American Victories – Americans capture Sedan.
French capture Rethel in the Bourgogne*

November 7 - 11

Germany negotiates an armistice with the Allies in Ferdinand Foch's railway carriage headquarters at Compiegne

November 7

New State Bavaria in Southern Germany is declared a German Republic

November 9

New Leader Kaiser Wilhelm II abdicates Max Ebert replaces Crown Prince Max as Chancellor of Germany

November 10

Kaiser Wilhelm II flees to Holland with Crown Prince Max

November 10

German republic is founded

English and French. French cavalry, Americans, guns, hundreds of them.

5th – 6th November

Had taken over limber gunners job. Went into ordnance for adjustments to "air buffer." Near Cortrai, in an old brewhouse. Village bombed. Civilians in house opposite killed.

7th November

Work on gun. Packed up. Back to wagon line. Through Cortrai and Gullegem to Wellegem (Wevelgem). Billet in house. Visited German Bakehouse.

8th November

Cleaning up, and at night moved nearer line. All quiet.

9th November

Went further up. A few guns could be heard a long way to our right.

10th November

Moved on, and were told that at midnight we were going on. Tomorrow would commence the "big Push". We were looking forward to it and that night at 10 p.m, we saw a blaze of lights behind us. Rockets. Phone message came through to return. The war had finished.

Back we went. That night us gunners never got further than Cortrai. What a night.

11th November

We washed the guns down. Football match and more celebrations.

12th and 13th November

Painted guns and wagons. We were to march through Belgium.

14th November

Moved off 10 a.m. Through Harelbeke, passed position of October 30th. Stayed near windmill position. Billet in barn. We were following the Germans back. Two days march in between.

15th November

Moved off 8 a.m. Through Inooigem, crossed Schelde. Bridges destroyed. Roads mined. No railways working. Ronse. Stayed just outside. Decent Town. Billet in barn. Frost. Beautiful night. Walked with Corporal C.... to little estaminet at La Houppe. Had a good night.

16th November

Cleaning up. Civilians returning from the East. Had been forced to work for the enemy in mines and factories. Walked to Luce Meanes in afternoon. (Louisa Maria, a small village in

November 11

Final Armistice Armistice Day; General Armistice is signed 5am. Fighting ceases at 11am

triangle of Ronse and La Houppe). Stayed the night at La Houppe.

17th November

Left section and went back to ....?

19th November

Rain, moved off 5 a.m. Snowed. Stayed at farm near Ninove. People were very good to us.

20th November

Cleaned up

21st November

Moved off 7 a.m. Damp day. Stayed night at Gooik. Good sized village. I was on picquet. Sergeant Clark informed me that I was to have a joy day in Brussels next day. What a night I had. Horse line gave way. One horse I lost. I searched for it for an hour or more. I suppose it was found. Well at 4 a.m, a party of us set out to catch a train at Lennock St Quentin, and to Brussels. What a day we had. First British to be seen in Brussels and first entry of the Royal Family since 1914 retreat. A huge procession. Bands playing everywhere. Where we went that day I do not know. (Several times have I been to Belgium since but have been unable to recognise anything familiar to the memories of that day) My bandolier was full of ammunition when I

arrived. I had not a single round left next day.
Wine was plentiful. Several went to dinner at
some "posh" house. Where I do not know – at night
every ally was represented. Arm in arm across the
wide Boulevards and all at once a section would
vanish into a café. Wine and champagne. Who
paid I do not know. I had more money when I
arrived back than I had when I started. Well, I
do not really remember going back except for
waking up at the platform at Lennock.

23rd November

Moved off 8 a.m. Many of those who went to
Brussels hadn't returned. St Job. Saw the
battlefield of Waterloo in the distance through
the forest of ..... a lovely place.

To some racing stables near Kveylast. Horses in
stables. Civilian beds. Guns on road.

24th November

Cleared up. Went to town at night. A lively time
with "Jocks" and civilians.

25th November

Moved off 7.30 a.m. Oyeau. Billet at mill.

26th November

Danced at night.

27th November

Off at 7, through Wavre on Namur Road. Stayed the night at Jouche. Billet in school. Good time with civilians.

28th November

Moved off 7 a.m along the Liege road. Night in barn.

29th November

Off at 8 a.m through Amay along the banks of the ..... (Meuse) At the above town we were met by a civilian band. For miles they marched in front of our column. Factories all the way.

Stayed the night at Flemalle le Grand, 10 kilos from Liege. Billet in theatre. Our Major was one of the best. Major Andrews, a Scotchman about 30 years old. He had seen a good deal of fighting service. Had several decorations, and had been wounded on three occasions. He was liked by everyone. Instead of the gunners walking as in the 295th, gunners rode every inch of the way. During this march, he arranged that we should thoroughly enjoy ourselves. Billets couldn't have been better and it was always at a decent town or village where we halted. Even going out of our way to pass through big towns. He too enjoyed the experience.

The order of march was ten minutes halt every hour. That always was so. During this March we always halted in a village or town. What times we had with the civilians at these halts. Coffee – have never drunk so much before. Coffee was brought to us at every halt. Our gun was decorated with evergreens and flags. The civilians had done this. More like a moving Christmas tree; and at the halt for the night, the civilians washed our guns down, and fetched water for the horses. Helped the driver to groom down – And at night we were left to the "mercy" of the civilians. There were concerts, dances arranged etc. I know that I didn't buy many drinks. Several times had invitations out to tea, supper – every town and village was decorated. There was never such a time.

30th November

Still at Flemalle Le Grand
Cinema and Dance

1st December

Off at 8 a.m. Pretty country. To Nessonvaux. Met with band. Civilian billet.

2nd and 3rd December

Nessonvaux.

4th December

Through Liège to Verviers. Stayed the night.
Billet in school. A large town. Plenty of fun.

5th December

Off again. Major informed us that our holiday
was finished. Stripped guns of decorations. Loaded
rifles. At 11 a.m, crossed the frontier. A stone
marking the boundary on the slope of the hill. In
distance could see village. We wondered what it
was like. Passed through village. Tramlines.
Belgians were claiming horses from Germans. On
to Warheim. Stayed night in theatre. Two large
busts one of the Kaiser and one of Bismark. They
were quickly removed. (I remember the old
caretaker sweeping up the pieces) The drapings of
the stage came in hand(y) for towels.

6th December

On to Gressonich. Adventure in German House.

7th December

Stayed night at Duren.

8th December

A long march. Stayed the night at old Prisoner
of War camp at Benzelia. A bricket factory. Was
dark when we arrived. Groped around in the soot

and dust. When we got to the light we couldn't help laughing. Black as niggers. French has fight with McGary.

9th December

Off at 8 a.m. Into the suburbs of Cologne. A busy place. Went to cinema. Billet in house. Guns in sheds. Painted guns. A lively time at night. The Germans did not know what to make of them and we couldn't make much of them.

13th December

Moved off 8 a.m. Rain. Through Flora Cologne, and we crossed the Rhine. General Plummer took the salute at the bridge head. Stayed night at iron foundry at Weisdorf. Billet in Prisoner of War Camp.

14th December

Guns in factory. Buffing pole bars and other bright parts.

15th December

Off at 7 a.m. Oil Fields. Through Oplades Orlegs to Solingen. Pulled guns into brick factory in Bismarker Strasse. Billet above factory in Bismarker Place, opposite park.

And there we stayed until 19th April 1919.

January 10 - 15

Communist revolt in Berlin

January 18

Start of peace negotiations in Paris

January 25

Peace conference accepts principle of a League of Nations

February 6

German National Assembly meets in Weimar

February 14

Draft covenant of League of Nations completed

Solingen, the Sheffield of Germany. Most amiable we found the civilians. Special hotels and cafes for our use. Best seats in theatres and cinemas reserved for us. No charge on trams. This being so, we did some travelling. Saturdays and Sundays, I did no duties.

The great Swimming Bath was at our disposal. A route march twice a week. No drill or gunnery, only cleaning up. And guns and harness were spotlessly clean. Civilians had many restrictions. Had to be indoors at 8 p.m Anyone seen on the streets after that hour were arrested. All had to remove their hats at passing of Colours which were carried on every route march. Those failing to do so were arrested and marched in rear of column, up before a court and fined heavily.

One incident of note: An infantry officer was found stabbed. A man hated by his men. Still the Germans were blamed for this outrage. The result was that an immense fine was levied on the civilians, and they had to be in their houses an hour earlier. As to the civilians themselves, sure none of us could speak ill of them. Many a joke we had with their ex soldiers. Could hardly realise that only a few months ago we were fighting against them. The children and our lads became the best of friends.

Billets were comfortable. A huge gun shed was

built. And a shed inside for the limber gunner with chair, table and stove. A real holiday for us in the sheds.

Sports were arranged. Football matches, boxing contests, Concerts etc. Jimmy French (Hitchen) was trainer for the boxers. The ring was a haunt of mine.

19th April

Left Solingen 8 a.m. Tram from Kaisersall to Orligs Reception Camp. Paid 200 f. Train to Koln. No 1 Concentration Camp. Being old German barracks in town.

Dom - Cinema

20th April, Easter Sunday.

Moved to Weger Strasse. Tram rides down to Bonn. Back at 3 p.m. Down to Flora and Kalk Fair. Zoo. A good time in the beer gardens. Concert in the Hoch Strasse at night.

21st April

Street train to Bruelk. Walked to Knesburg Bahnhof. Met H Foster. Back to Koln. To Mulhelm Flora. Saw "Clinies" at the Apollo Theatre.

22nd April

Parade at 8.30. Embarked on river steamer Gotha. Grand day. Through Dusseldorf. 5 p.m.

arrived Lichenich, last German Town. Spent night on barge in middle of Rhine. Concert on board.

23rd April

Up at six. Off again. Picked up Dutch Pilot at .... Tulips, Windmills, sand dredging. Rotterdam. On barge, towed under bridges to sheds other side of town. Good dinner (not of army style). Beds with white blankets. Three of us "broke bounds" went down in village.

24th April

4 a.m. embarked 12 hours trip. Cold voyage. Harwich. Liverpool Street.

AND SO ENDS MY DIARY.

May 6

Peace conference disposes of German colonies

May 7 - June 28

Treaty of Versailles drafted and signed

June 21

German High Seas Fleet scuttled at Scapa Flow

July 19

Cenotaph is unveiled in London

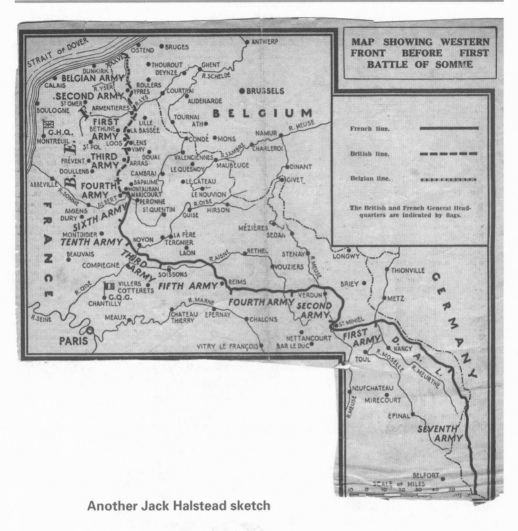

MAP SHOWING WESTERN FRONT BEFORE FIRST BATTLE OF SOMME

French line.	——————
British line.	— — — — —
Belgian line.	×·×·×·×·×·×·×

The British and French General Headquarters are indicated by flags.

Another Jack Halstead sketch

The following four pages have been reproduced directly from the diary

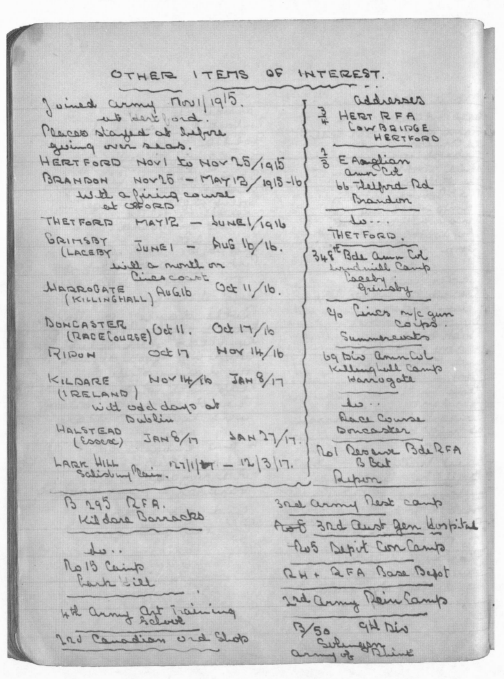

OTHER ITEMS OF INTEREST.

Joined army Nov1/1915.
     at Hertford.
Places stayed at before
     going over seas.
HERTFORD Nov1 to Nov 25/1915
BRANDON   Nov25 — MAY13/1915-16
     with a firing course
          at ORFORD
THETFORD   MAY12 — JUNE1/1916
GRIMSBY   JUNE1 — AUG16/16.
(LACEBY)
     with a month on
          Lincs court
HARROGATE AuG.16 Oct 11/16.
(KILLINGHALL)

DONCASTER Oct 11. Oct 17/16
(RACECOURSE)
RIPON   Oct 17   Nov 14/16
KILDARE   Nov 14/16 JAN 8/17
(IRELAND)
     with odd days at
          Dublin
HALSTEAD   JAN 8/17   JAN 27/17.
(Essex)

LARK HILL   27/1/17 — 12/3/17.
Salisbury Plain.

B 295 RFA.
   Kildare Barracks

do..

No 13 Camp
   Lark Hill

4th Army Art Training
          school
2nd Canadian ord Shob

Addresses
HERT RFA
   COW BRIDGE
        HERTFORD

E Anglian
   Ammn Col
66 Thetford Rd
     Brandon

do...
THETFORD.

348th Bde Ammn Col
   Lyndnill Camp
   Laceby
     Grimsby

c/o Lincs m/c gun
        corps.
   Summercoats

69 Div Ammn Col
   Killinghill Camp
   Harrogate

do..
Race Course
   Doncaster

No1 Reserve Bde RFA
   B Bat
     Ripon

3rd Army Rest camp

A of 3rd Aust Gen Hospital

No 5 Depot Con Camp

RH + RFA Base Depot

2nd Army Rein Camp

B/50   9th Div
     Cologne
   Army of Rhine

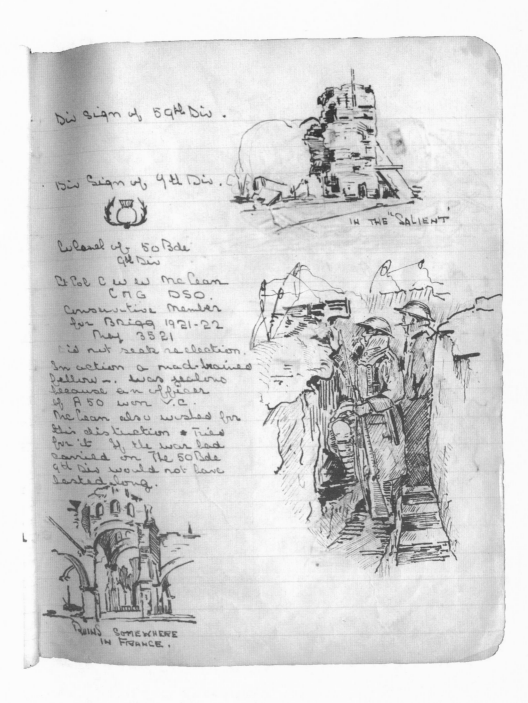

Div sign of 59th Div.

Div Sign of 4th Div.

Colonel of 50 Bde
9th Div

Lt Col C W W McLean
CMG DSO.
Conservative Member
for Brigg 1921-22
May 3521
did not seek re-election.

In action a mad-brained
fellow —. was jealous
because an officer
of A 50 won V.C.
McLean also wished for
this distinction & tried
for it. If the war had
carried on The 50 Bde
9th Div would not have
lasted long.

IN THE "SALIENT"

RUINS SOMEWHERE
IN FRANCE.

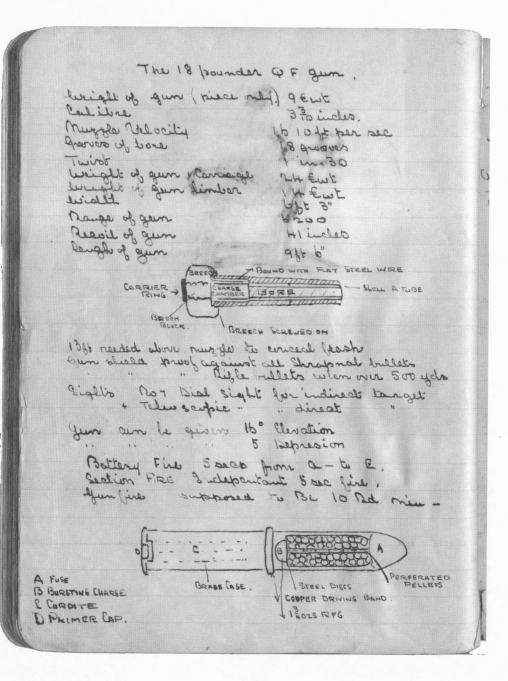

The 18 pounder Q F gun.

Weight of gun (piece only) 9 Cwt
Calibre   3 3/10 inches.
Muzzle Velocity   1b 10 ft per sec
Grooves of bore   18 grooves
Twist   1 in 30
Weight of gun & Carriage   24 Cwt
Weight of gun limber   14 Cwt
Width   6 ft 3"
Range of gun   6200
Recoil of gun   41 inches
Length of gun   9 ft 6"

13 ft needed above muzzle to conceal flash
Gun shield proof against all Shrapnel bullets
    "   "   "   Rifle bullets when over 500 yds
Sights   No 7 Dial Sight for indirect target
         + Telescopic   "   " direct   "
Gun can be given 16° Elevation
    "   "   "   "   5 Depression
Battery Fire 5 secs from a to E.
Section Fire Independant 5 sec fire.
Gun fire   supposed to Be 10 Rd min—

A FUSE
B BURSTING CHARGE
C CORDITE
D PRIMER CAP.

BRASS CASE.

STEEL DISCS
COPPER DRIVING BAND.
1 3/40 OZS RFG

PERFERATED PELLETS

SHELLS.

Various types used.
Shrapnel. with either
85 or 80 fuse
High Explosive
   Delay & Non delay

A Delay would hit a
wall – go through it
and burst in the room
The later would burst
on pressure
The Time High Explosive

The 106 fuse High Explosive
would burst on hitting
water. These shells
first used Sept 1917.

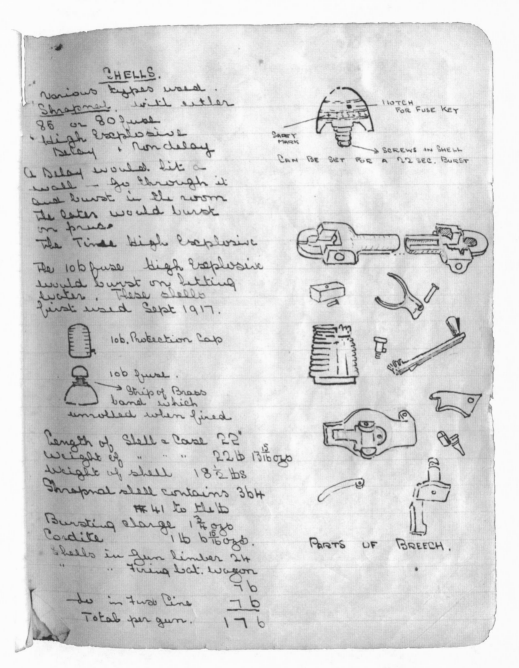

NOTCH FOR FUSE KEY

SAFETY MARK

SCREWS IN SHELL

CAN BE SET FOR A 22 SEC. BURST

106. Protection Cap

106 fuse.
→ Strip of Brass band which unrolled when fired

Length of Shell & Case 22"
Weight of   "   "   22 lb 13$\frac{15}{16}$ozs
Weight of shell   18$\frac{1}{2}$ lbs
Shrapnel shell contains 364
        41 to the lb
Bursting charge 1$\frac{7}{8}$ ozs
Cordite   1 lb 6$\frac{15}{16}$ozs.
Shells in gun limber 24
   "   " firing bat. wagon
                76
-do in two line   76
Total per gun.   176

PARTS OF BREECH.

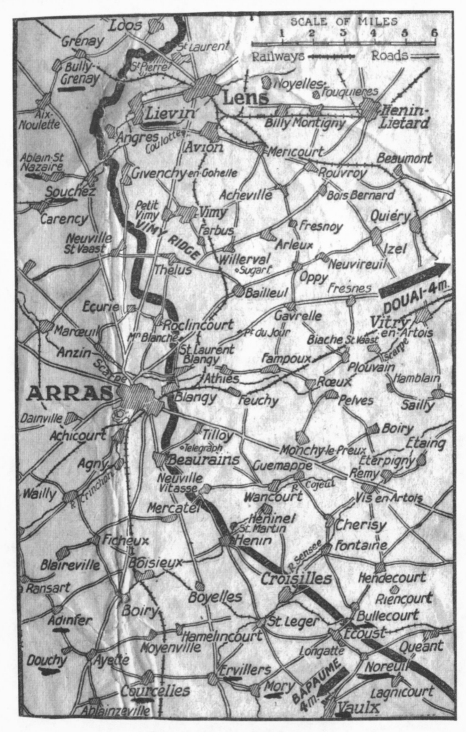

The final page in Jack's diary